Giant Adult Coloring Book

Over 100 Relaxing Mandalas to Color
One image per page

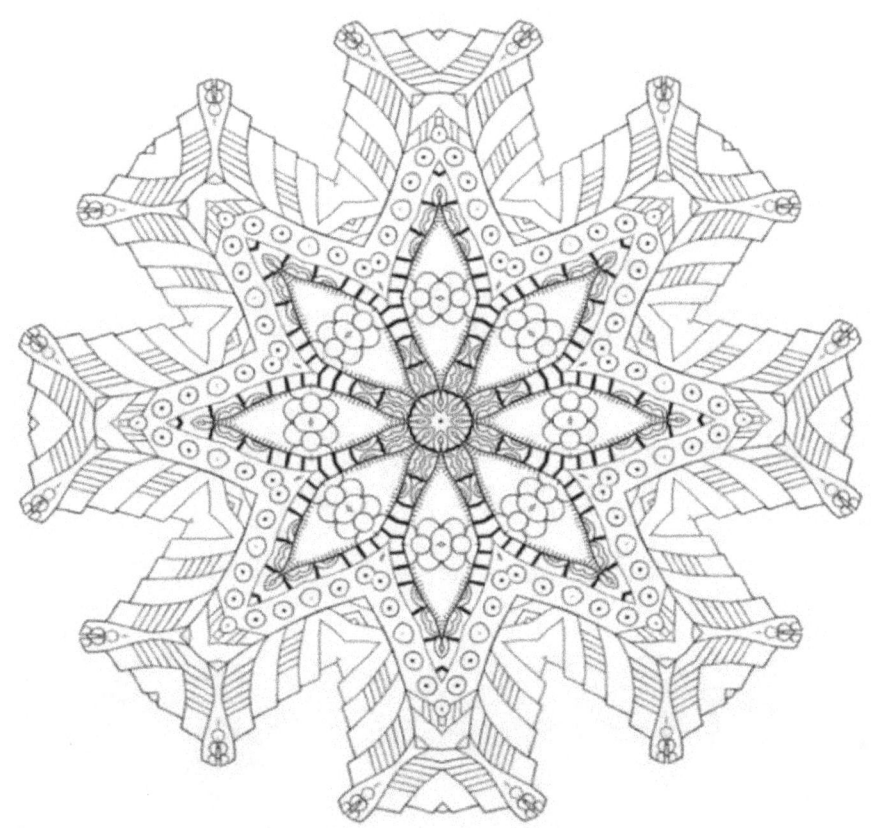

Go to: **www.calmdalas.com**
Get 10 **FREE** mandalas and be notified about new books!

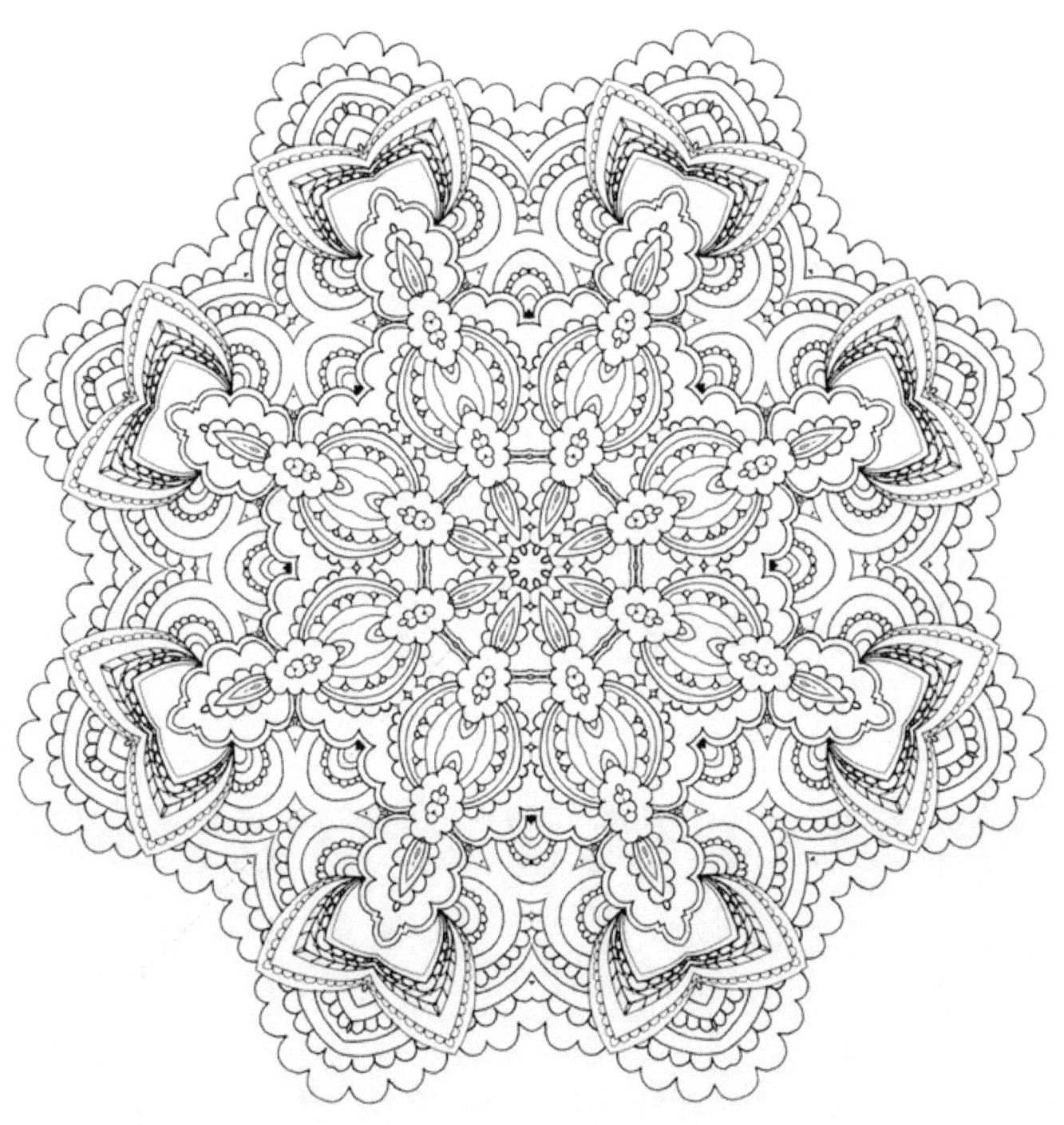

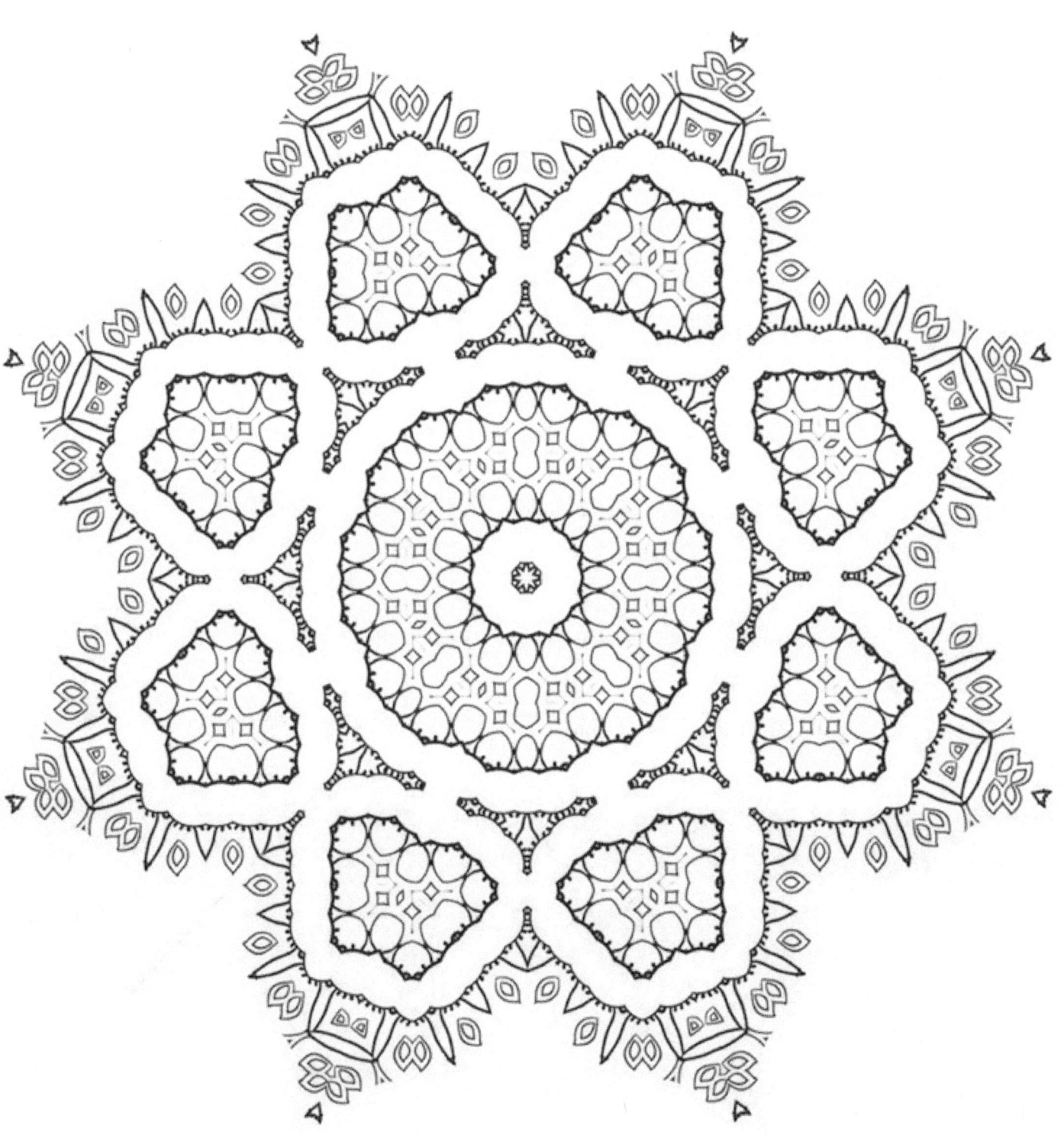

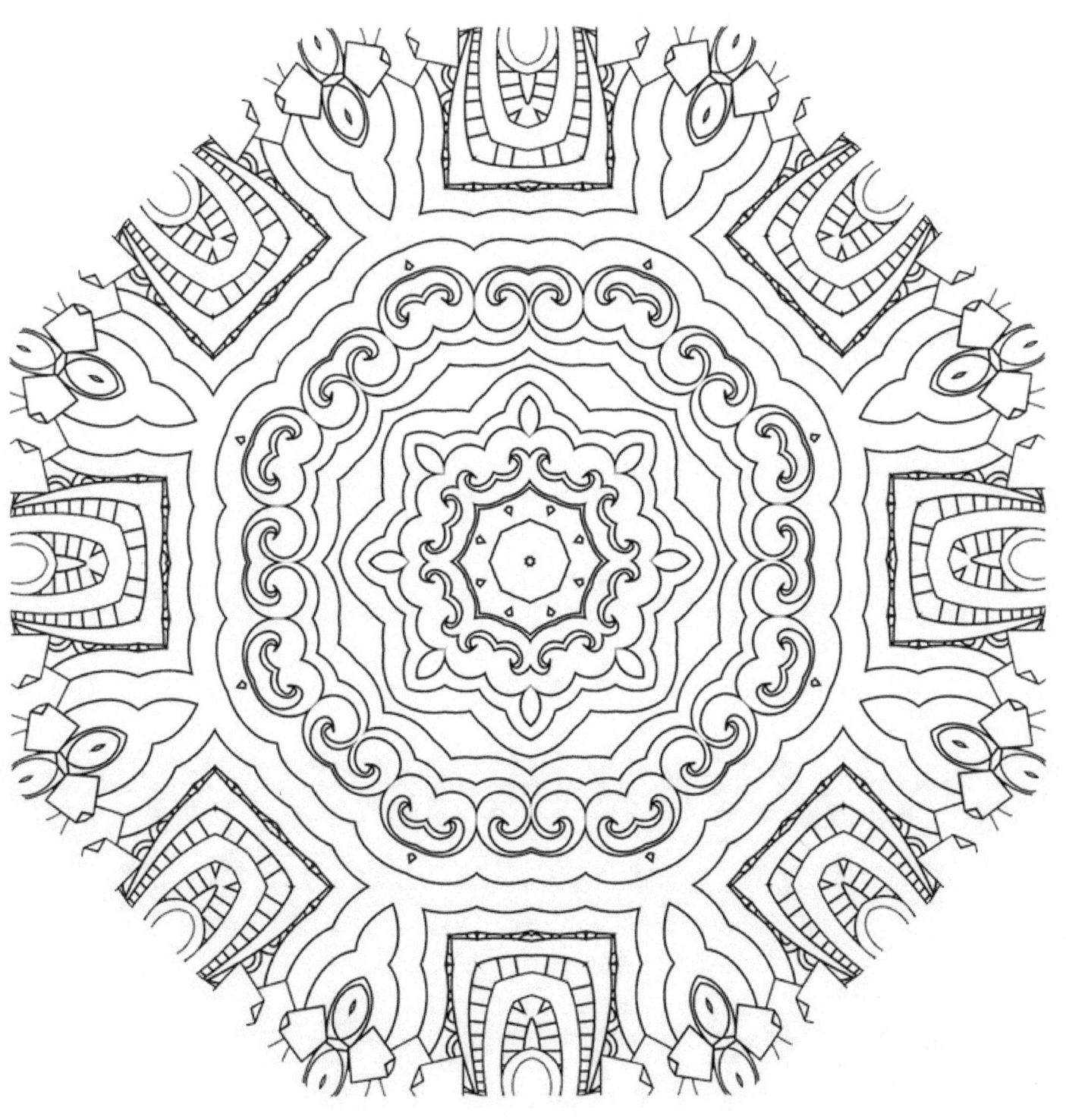

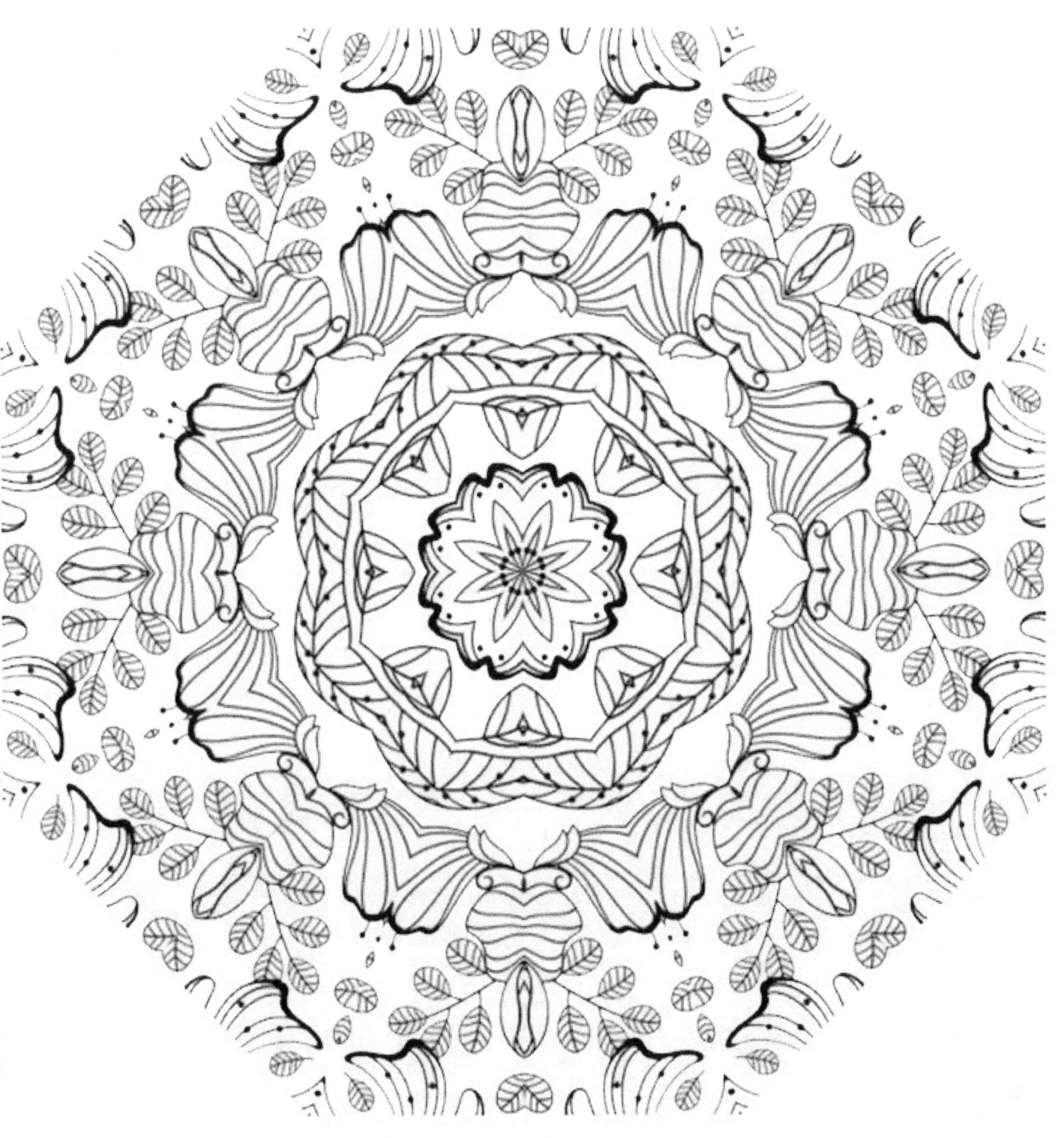

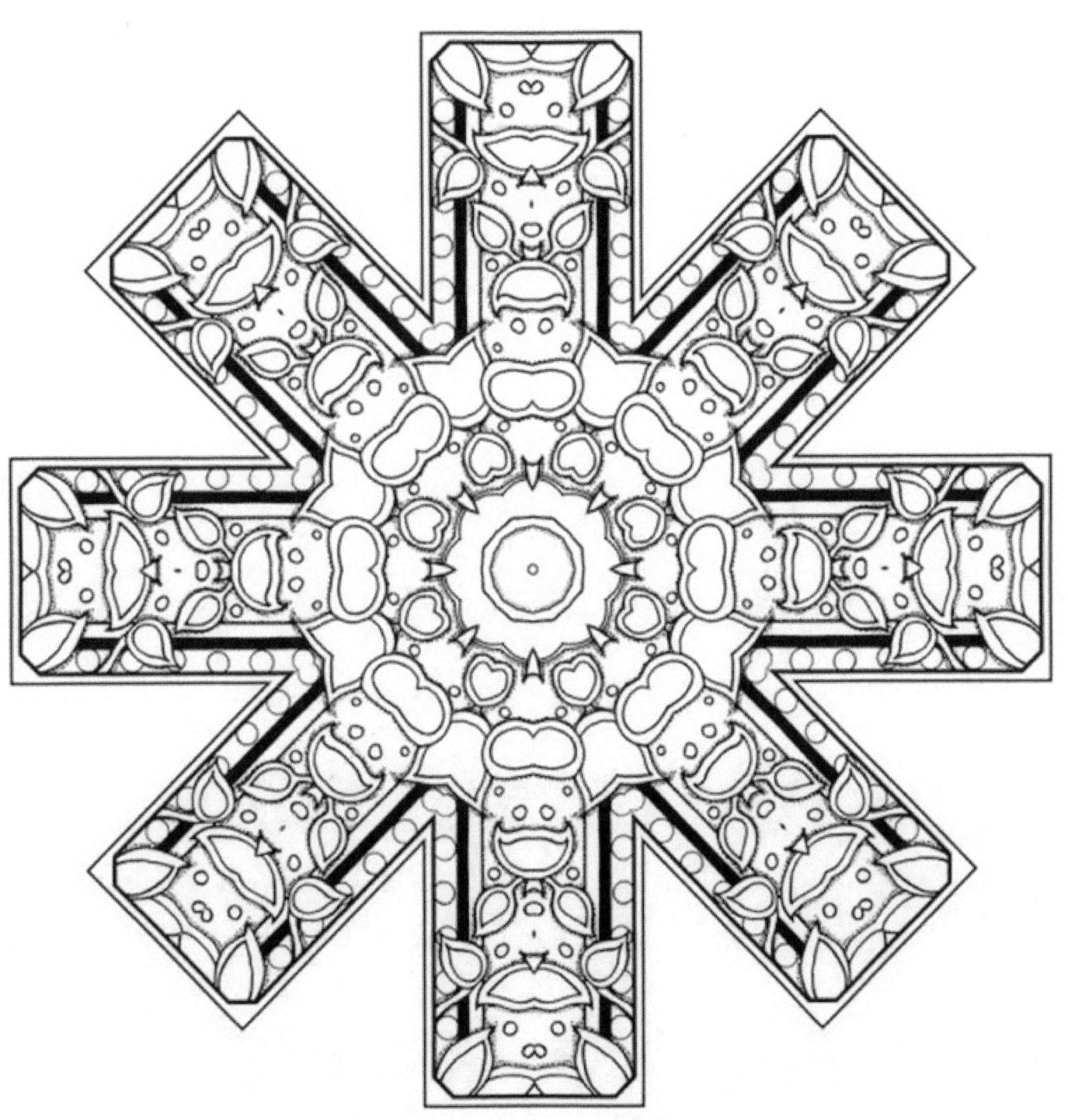

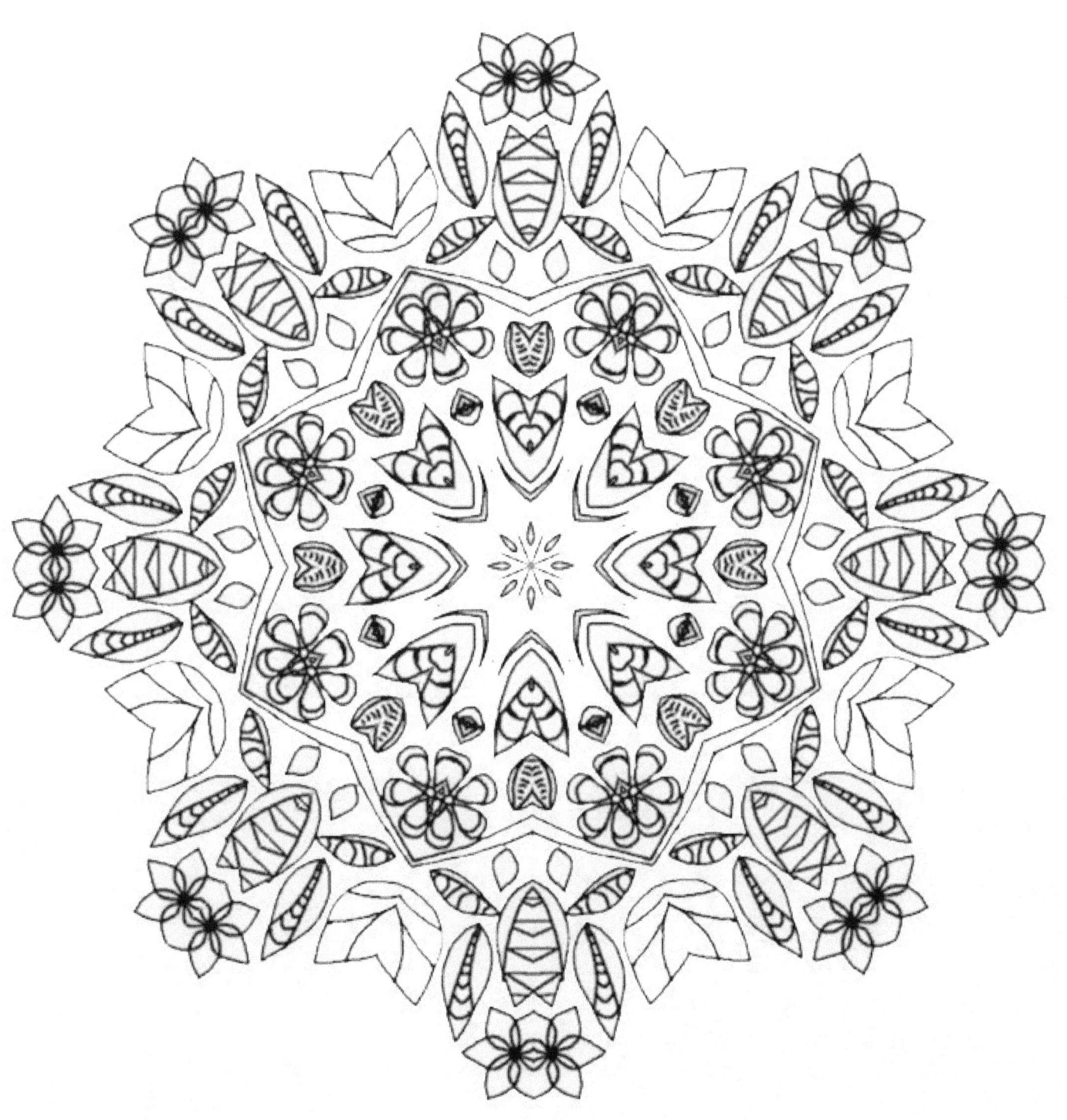

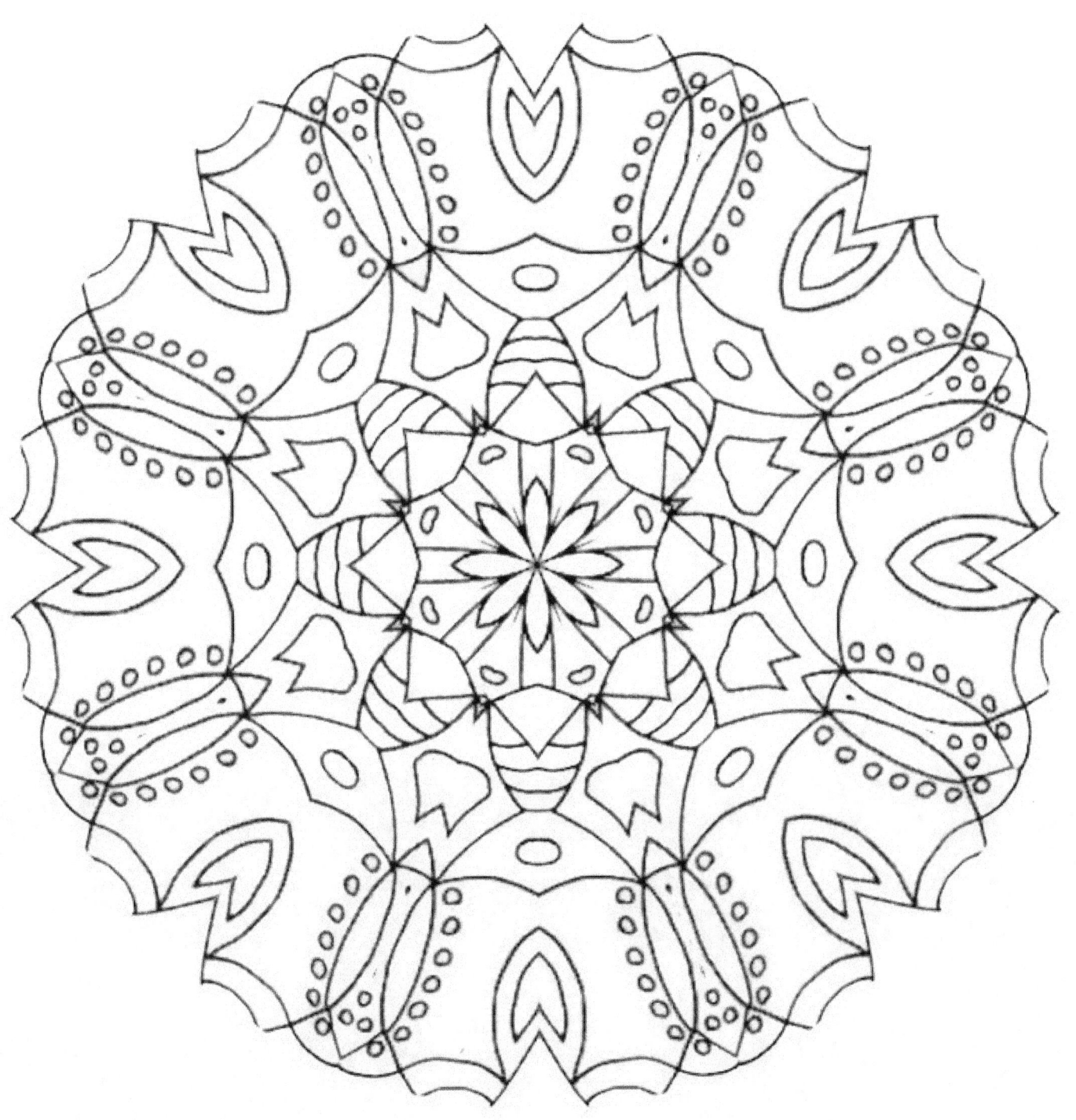

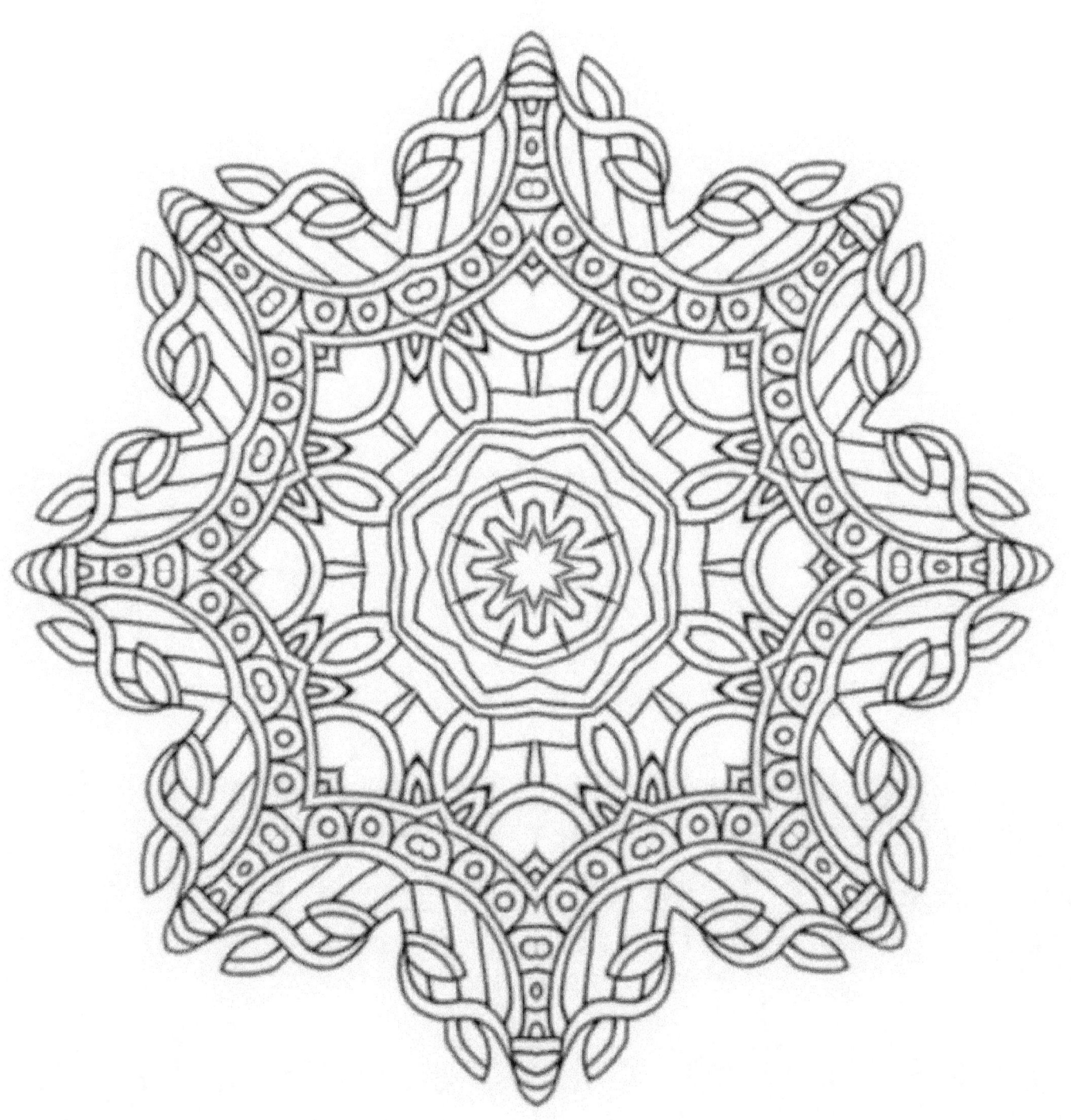

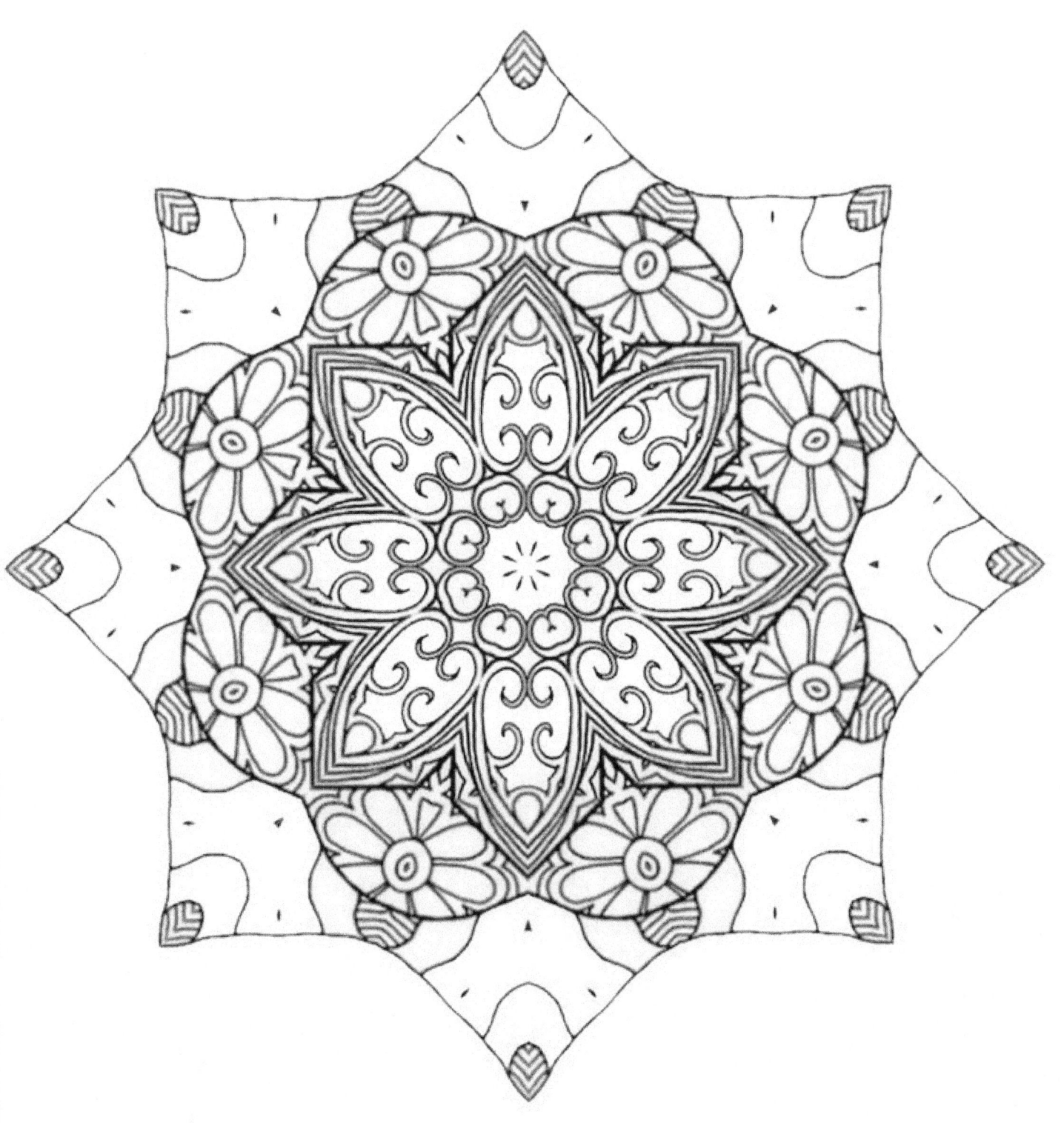

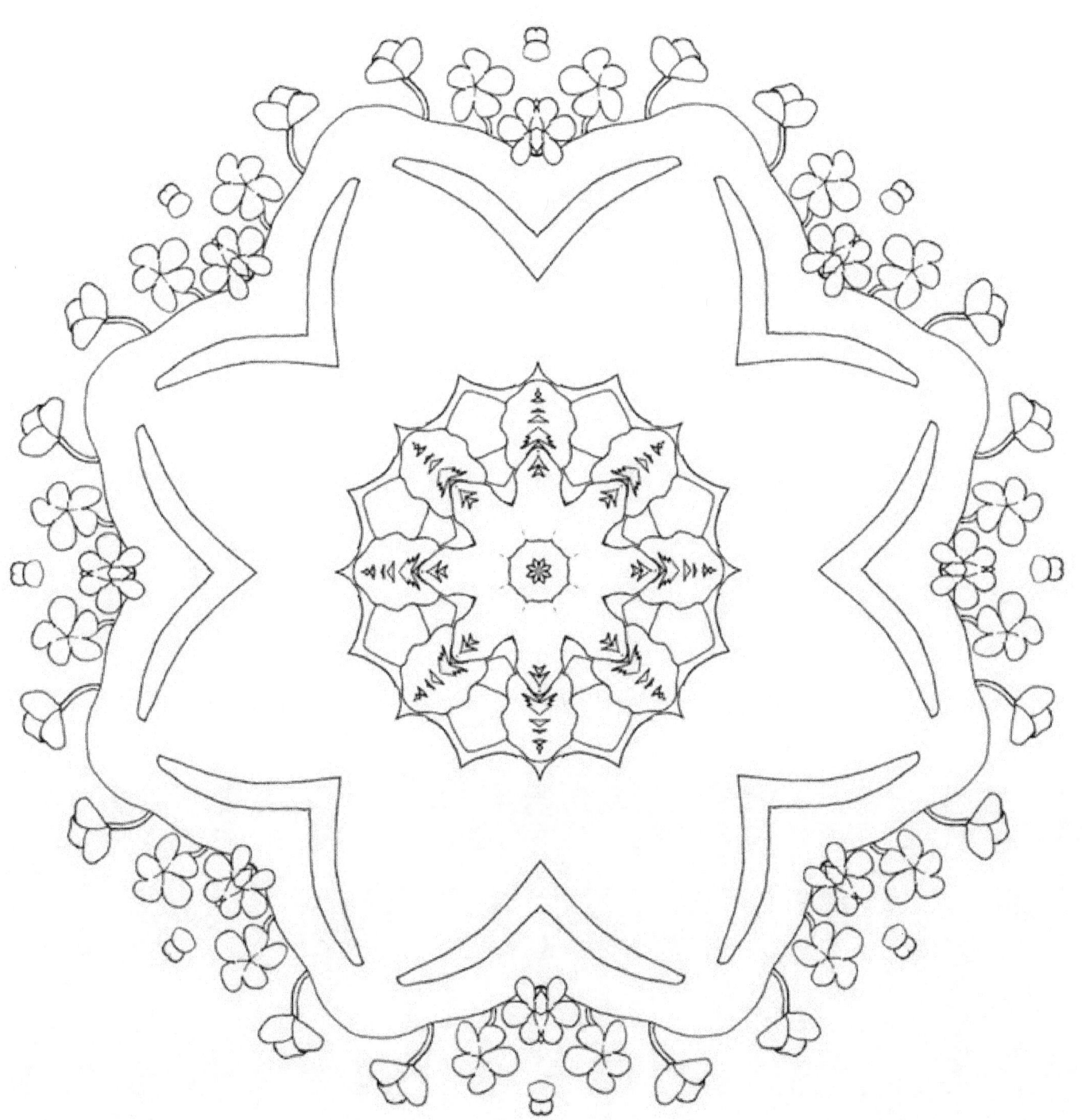

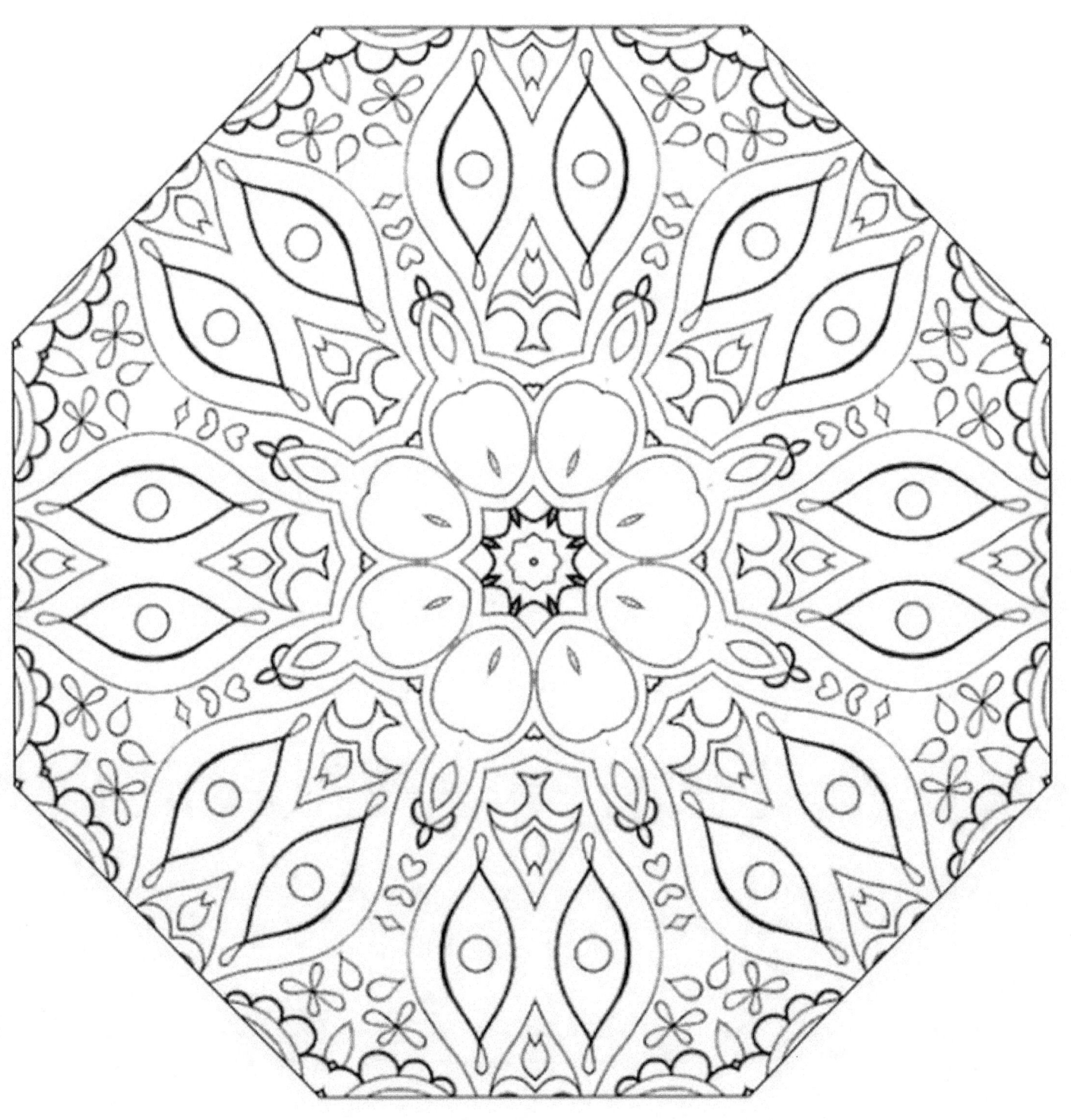

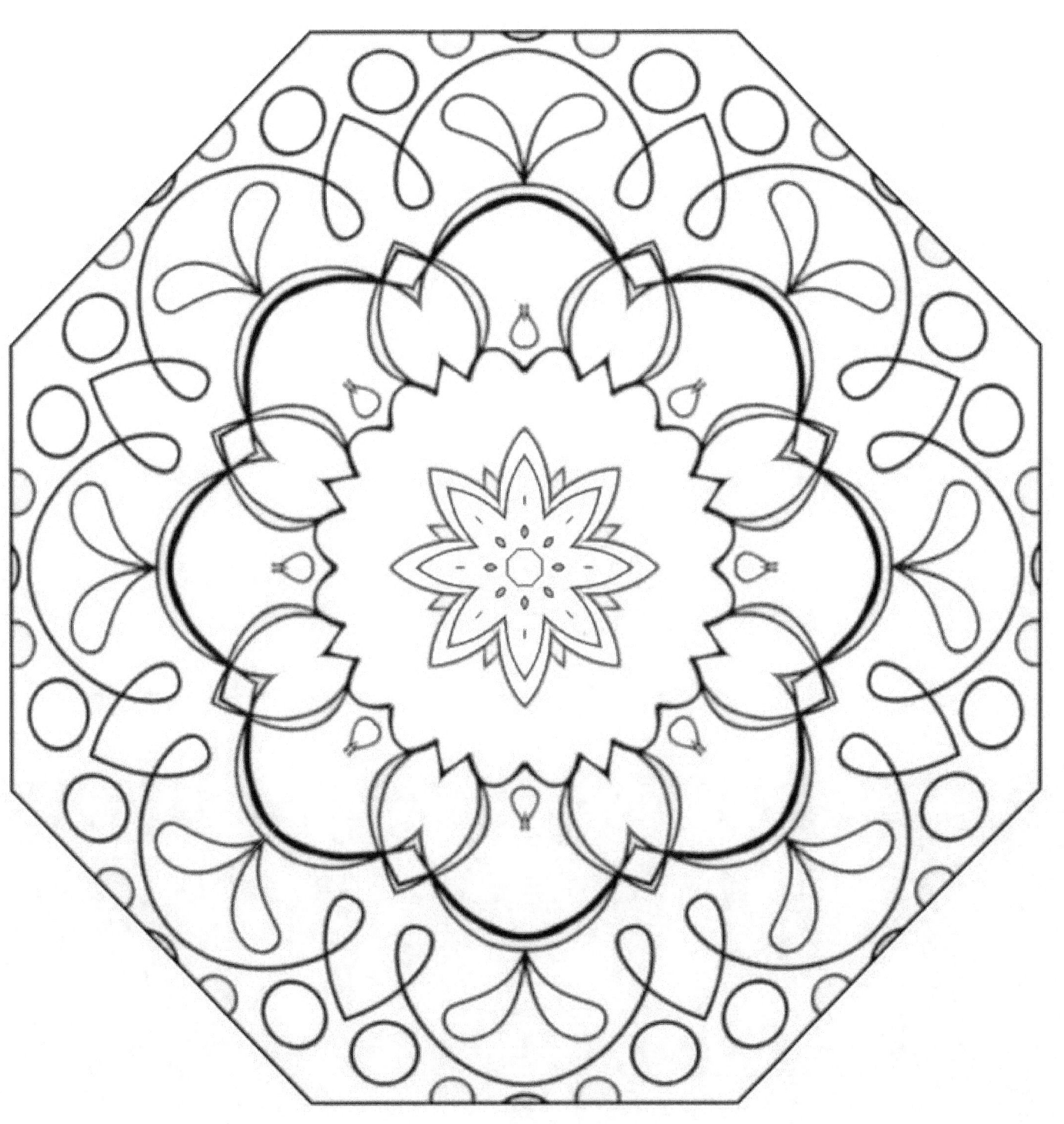

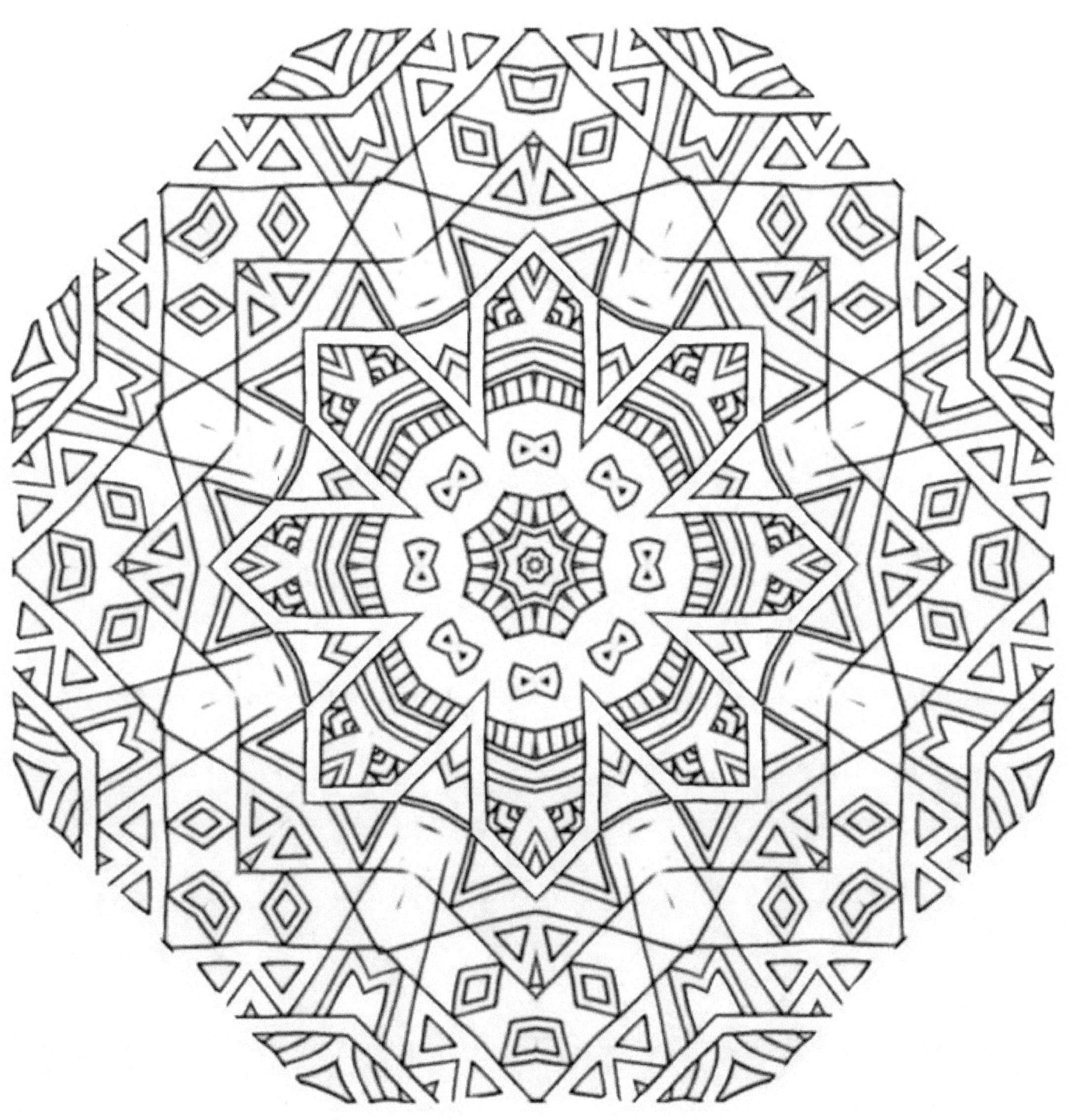

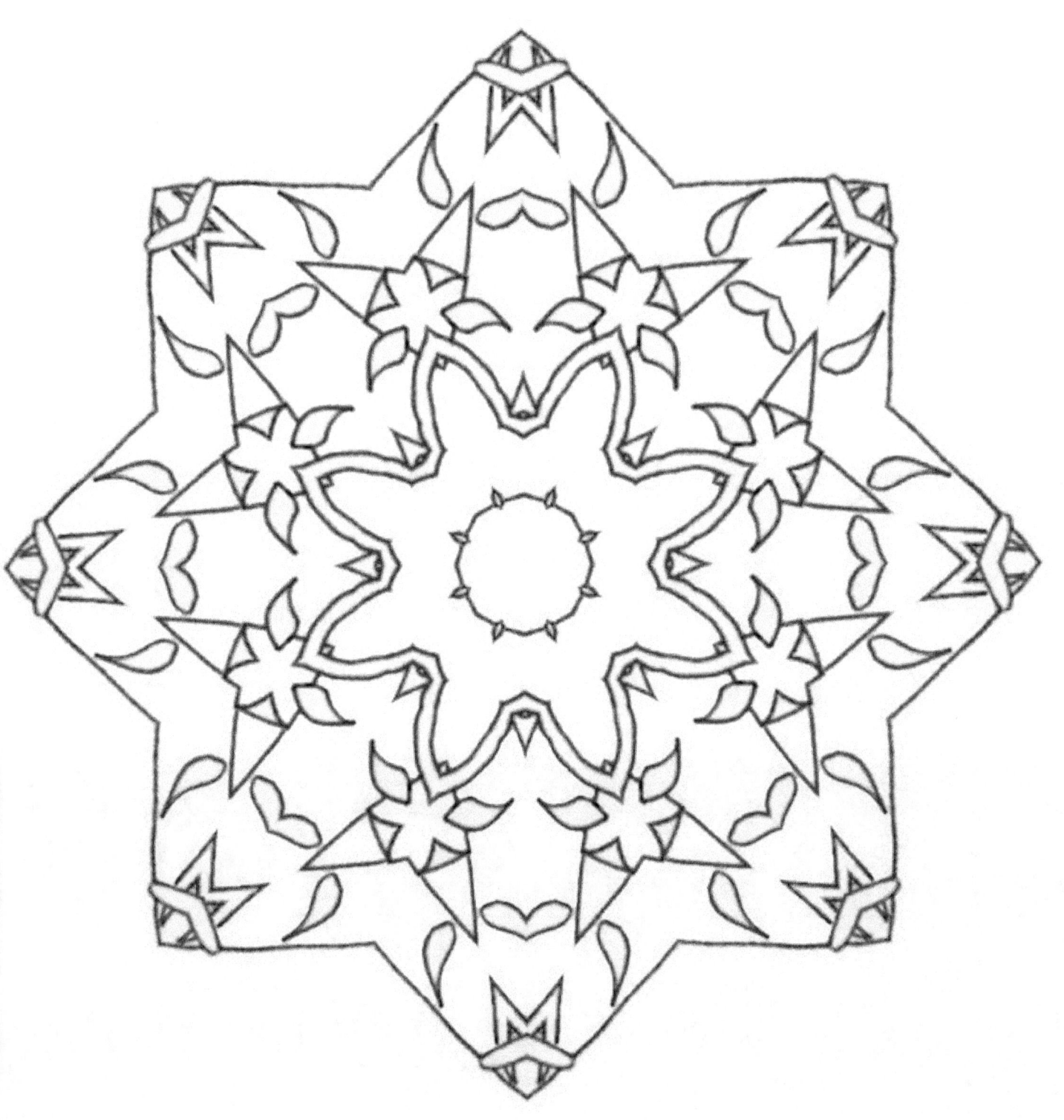

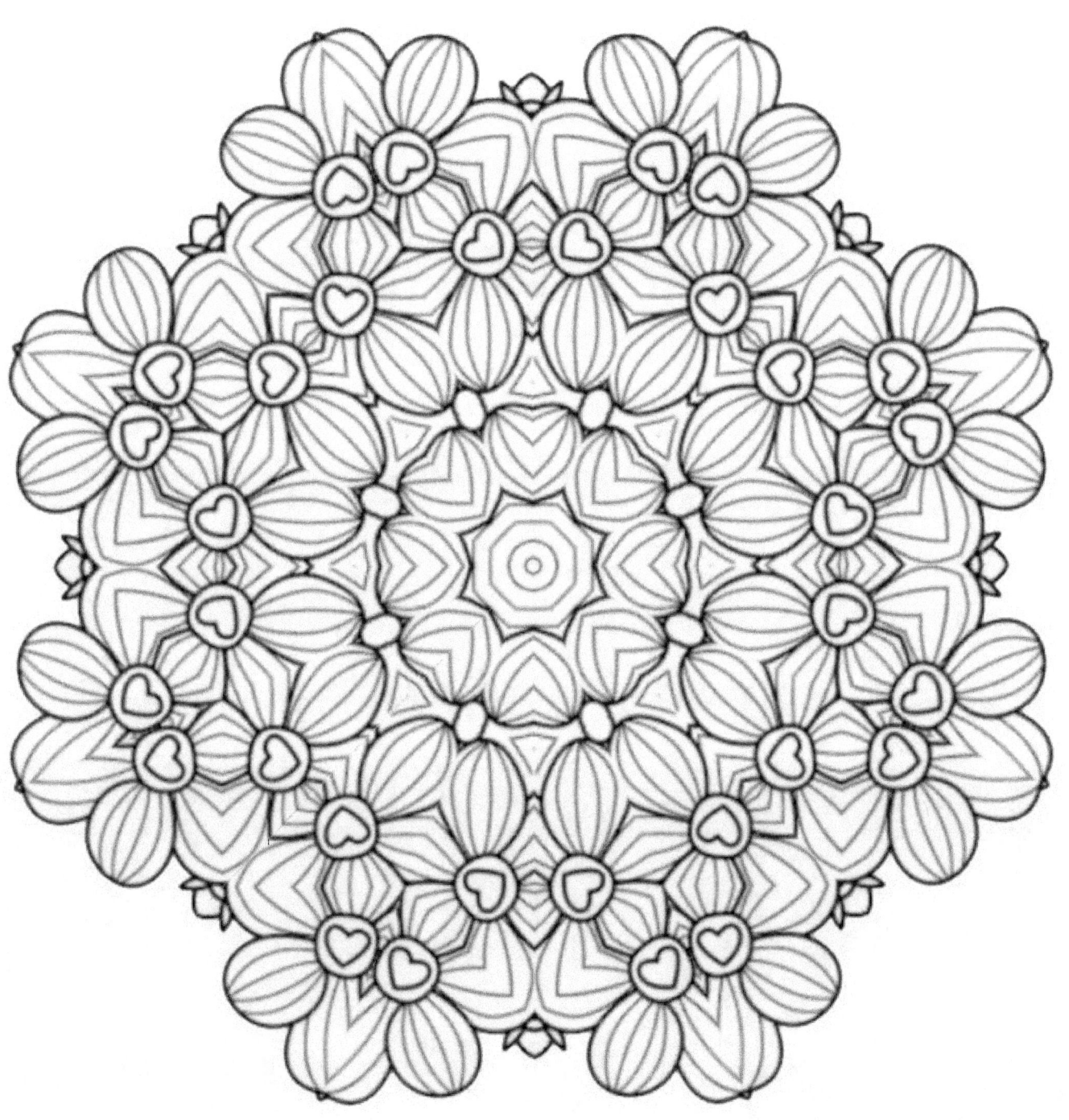

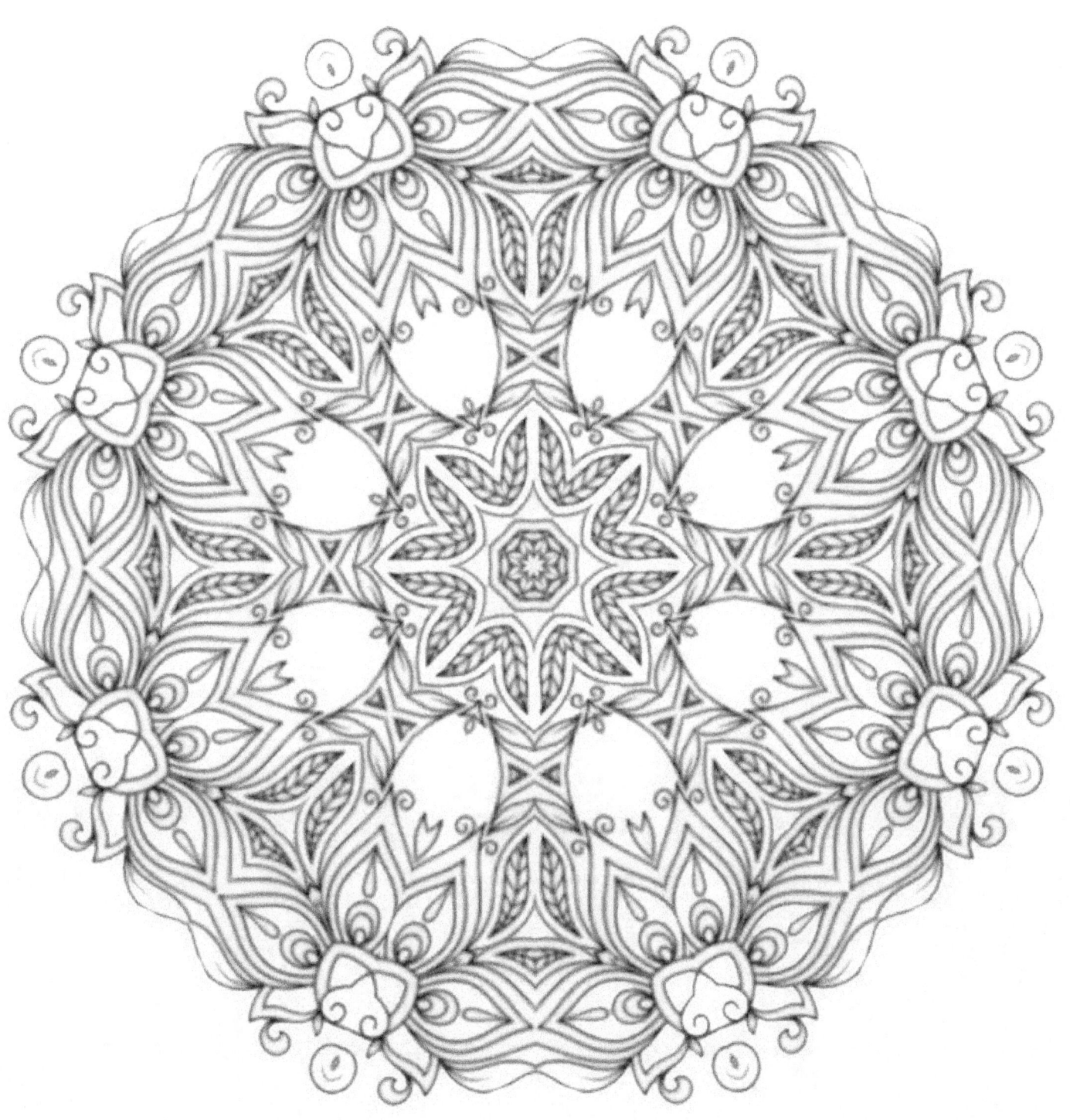

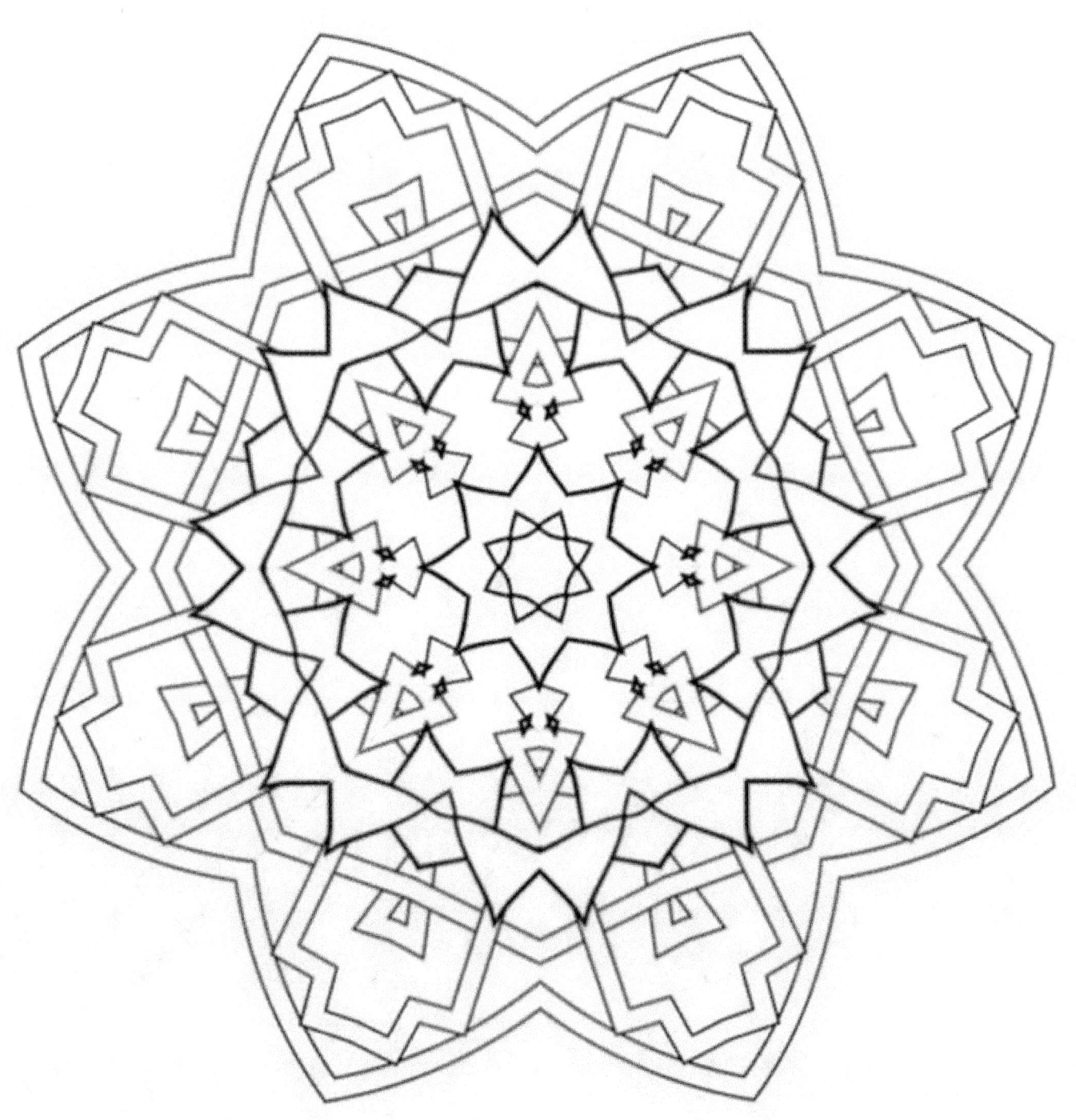

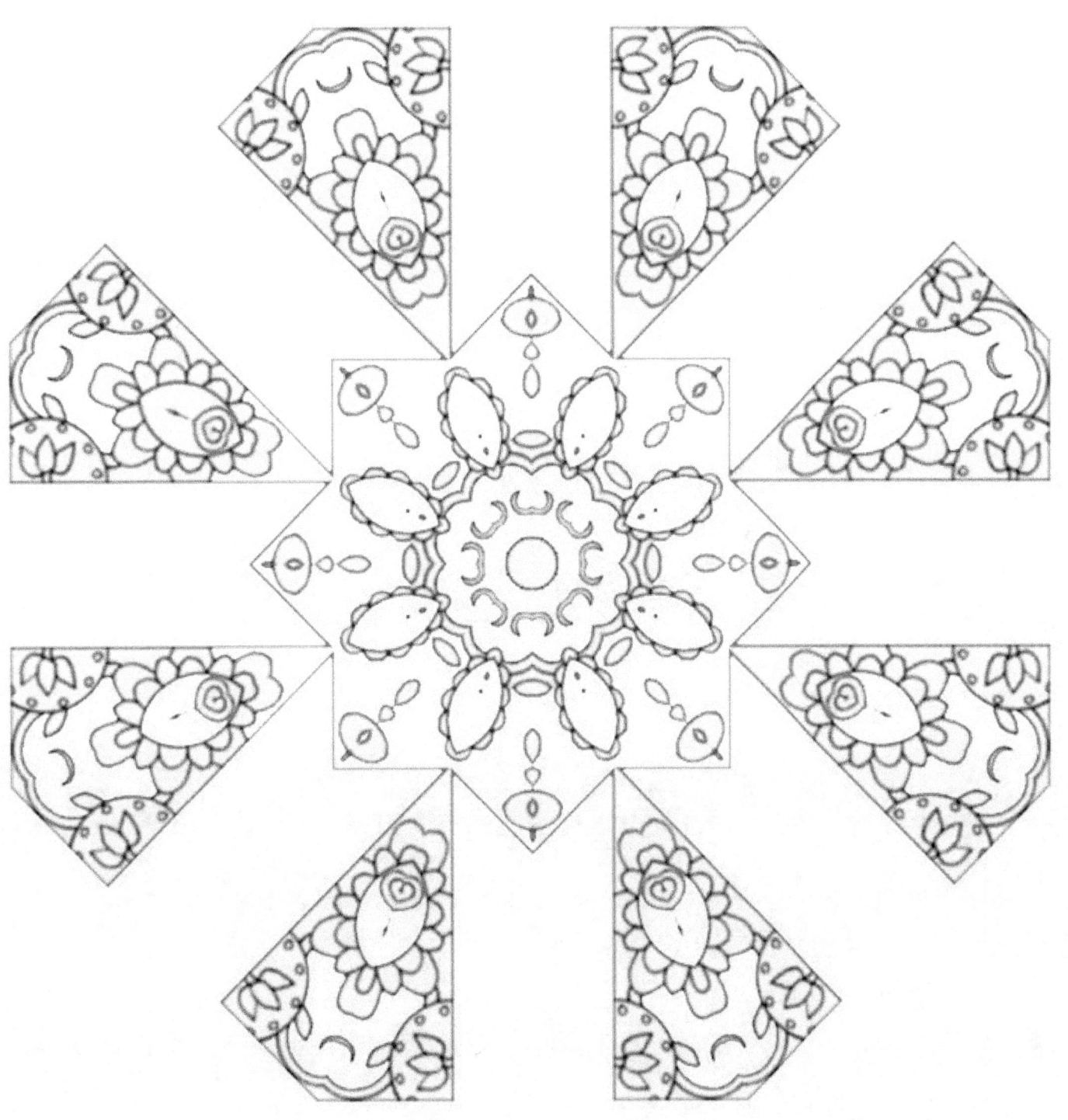

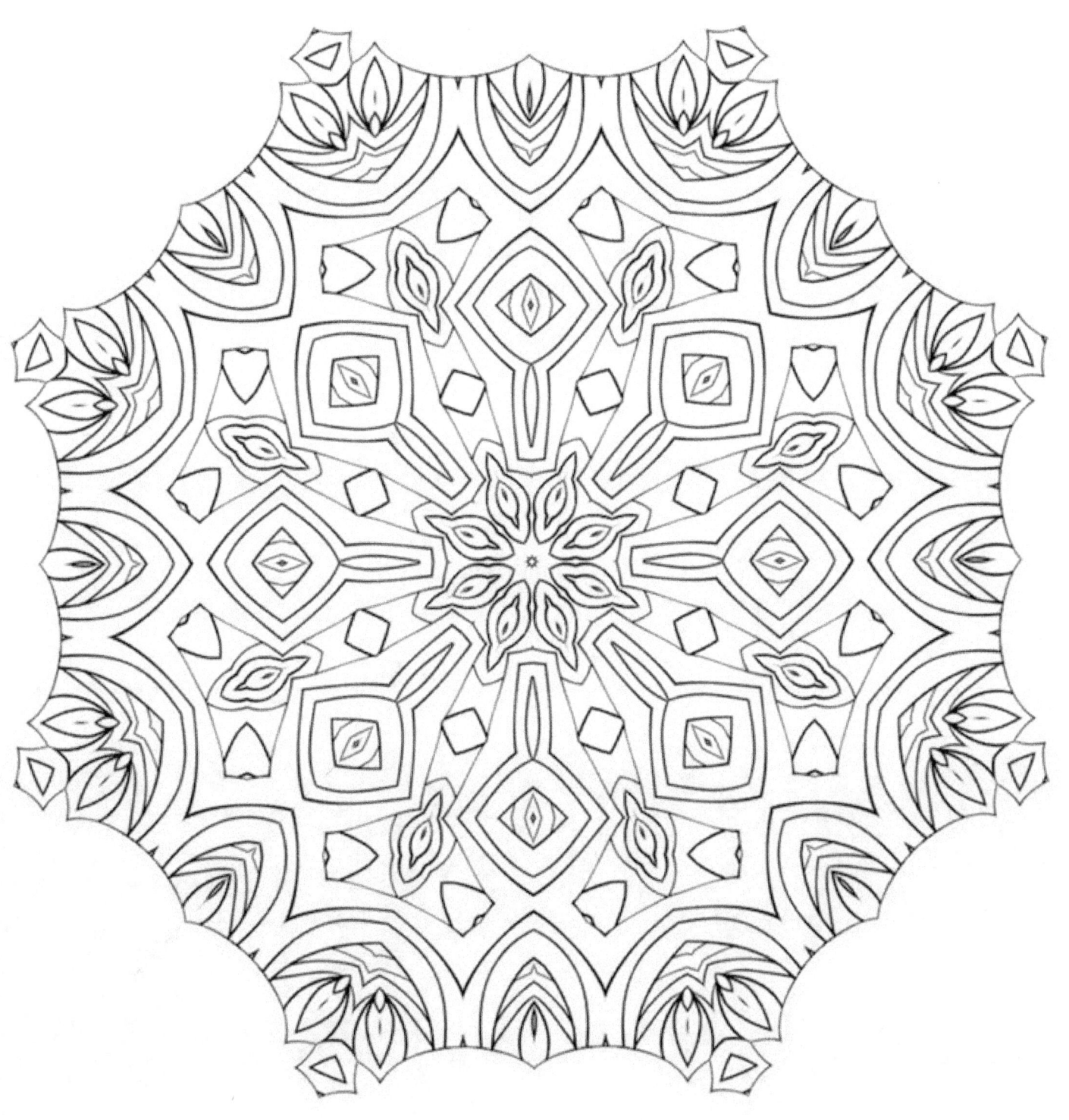

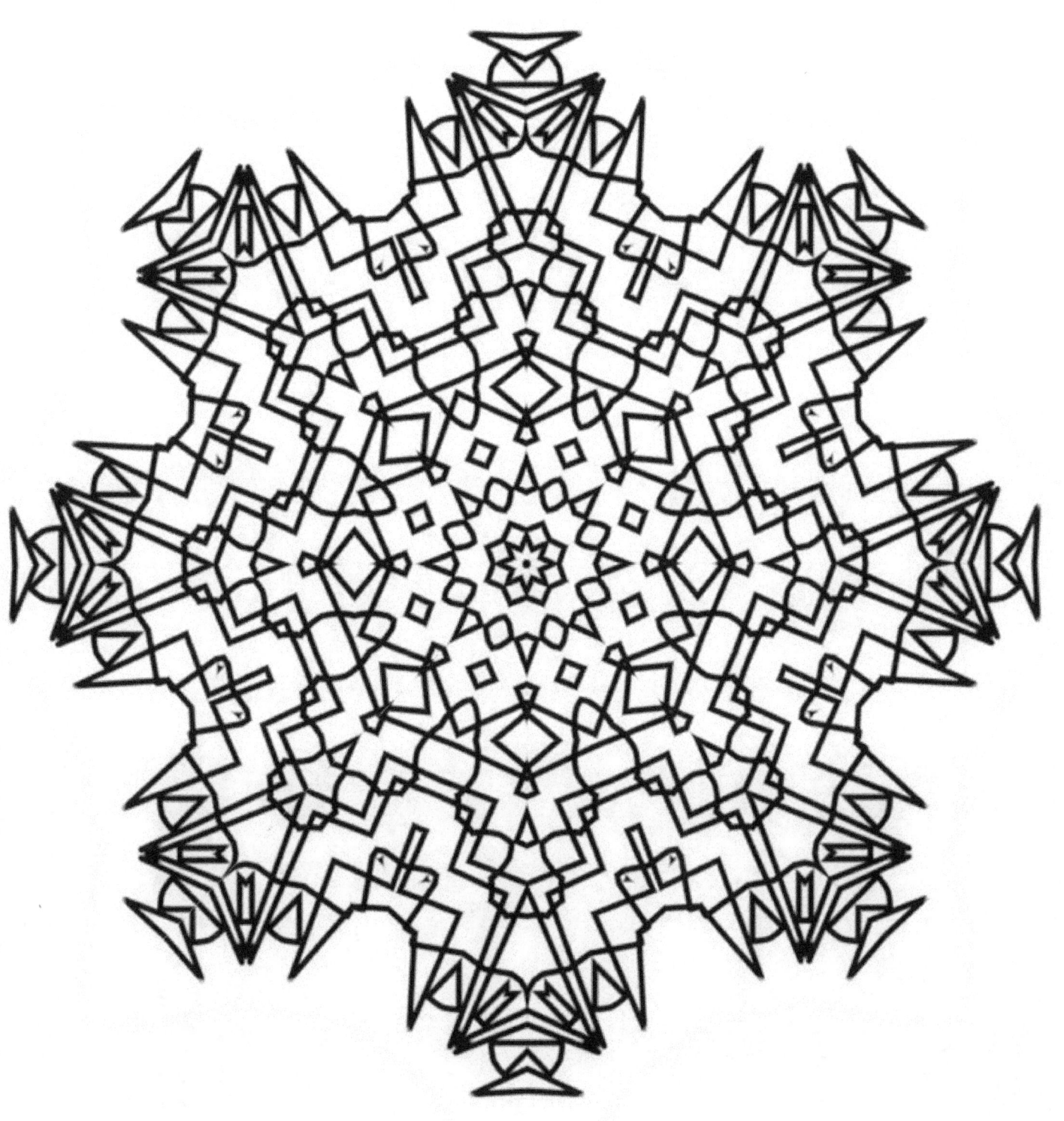

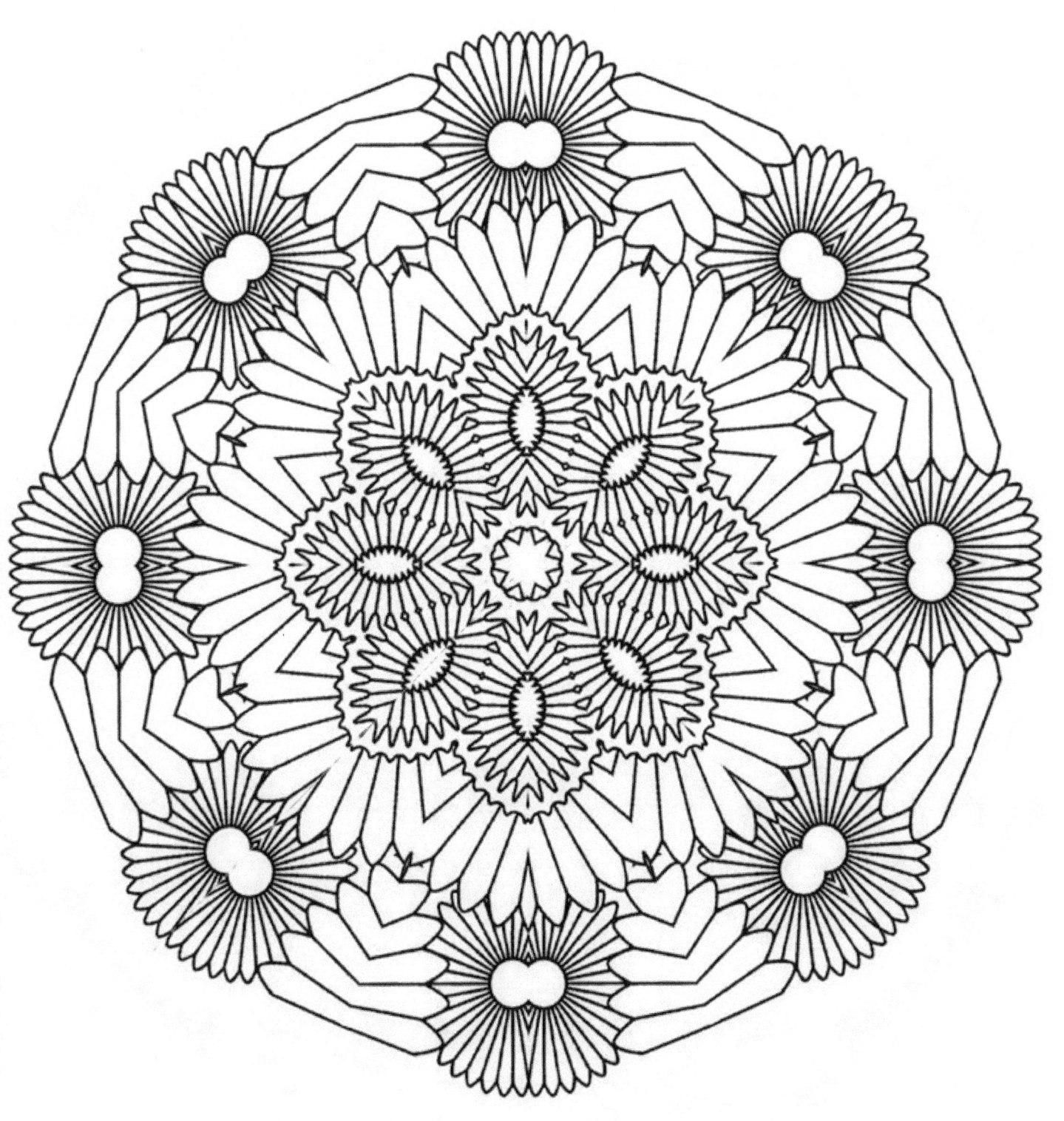

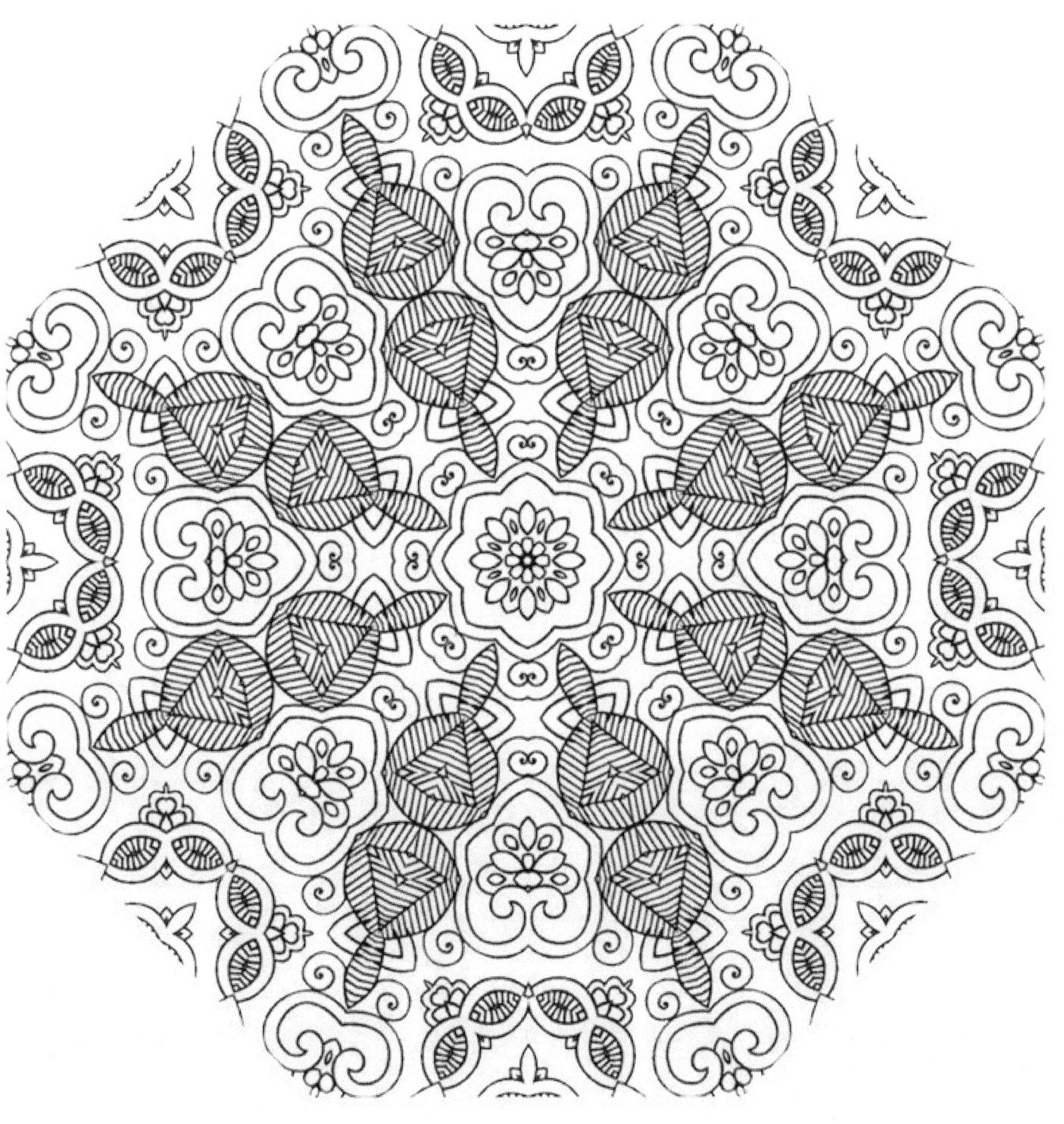

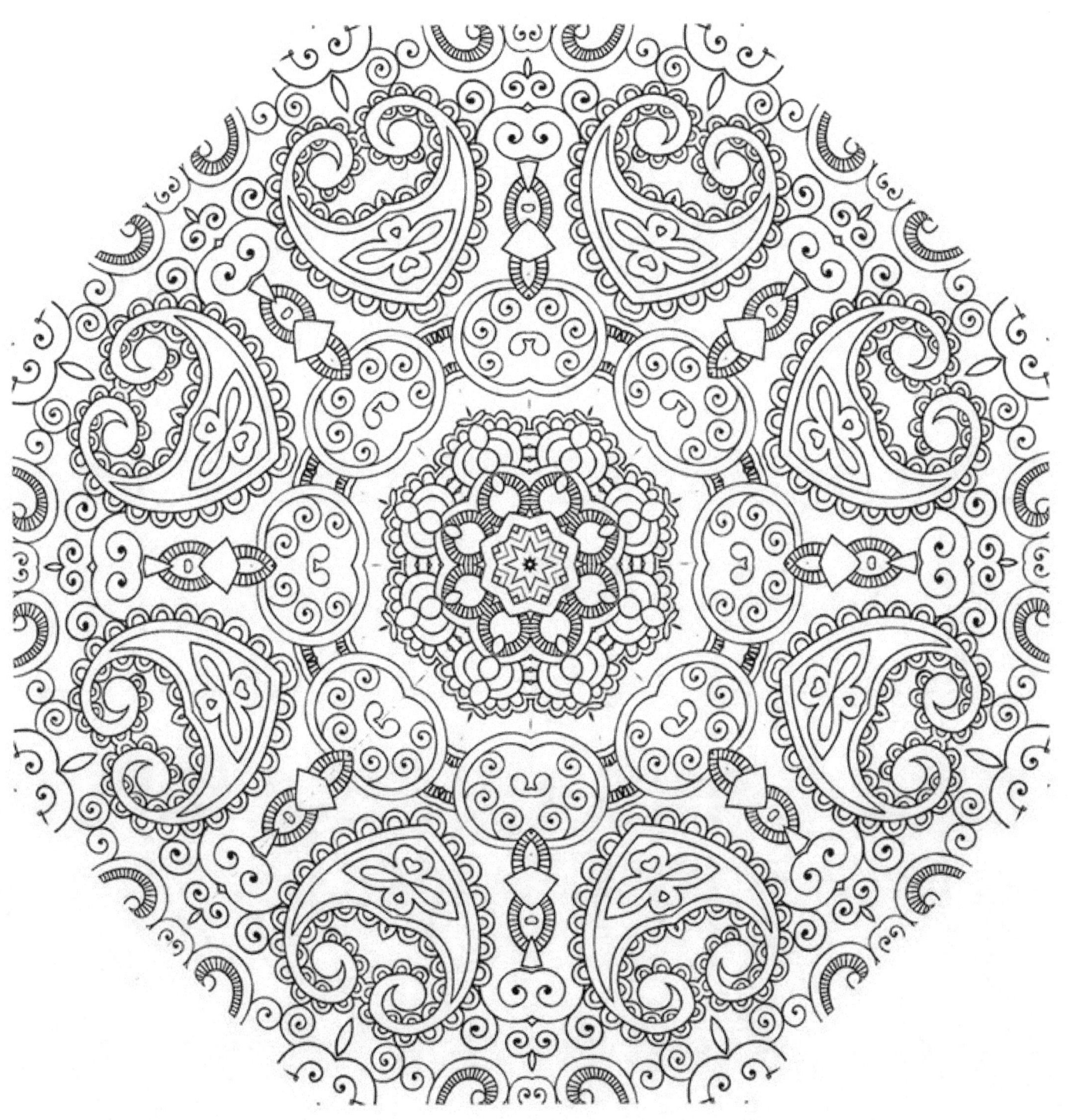

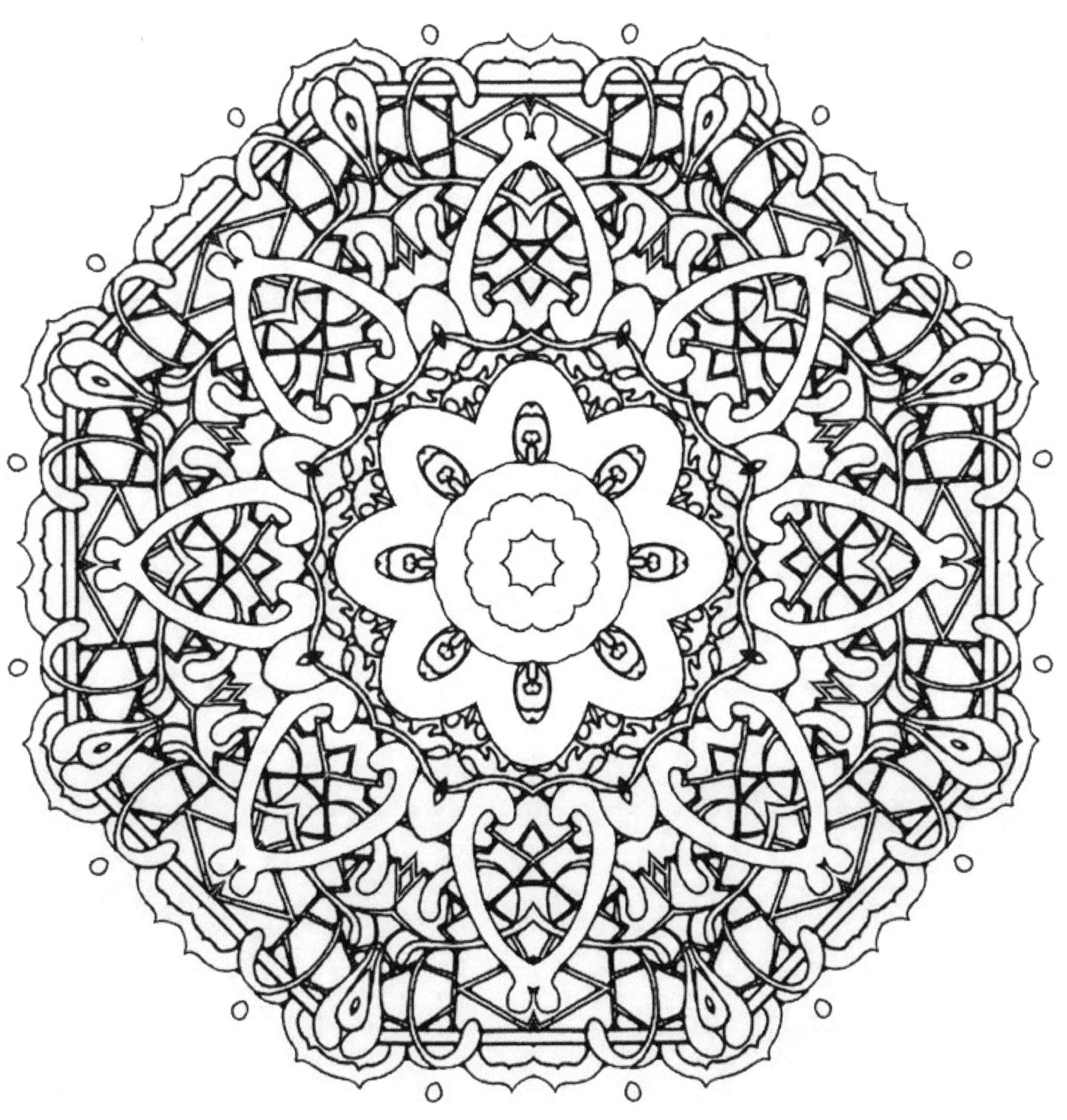

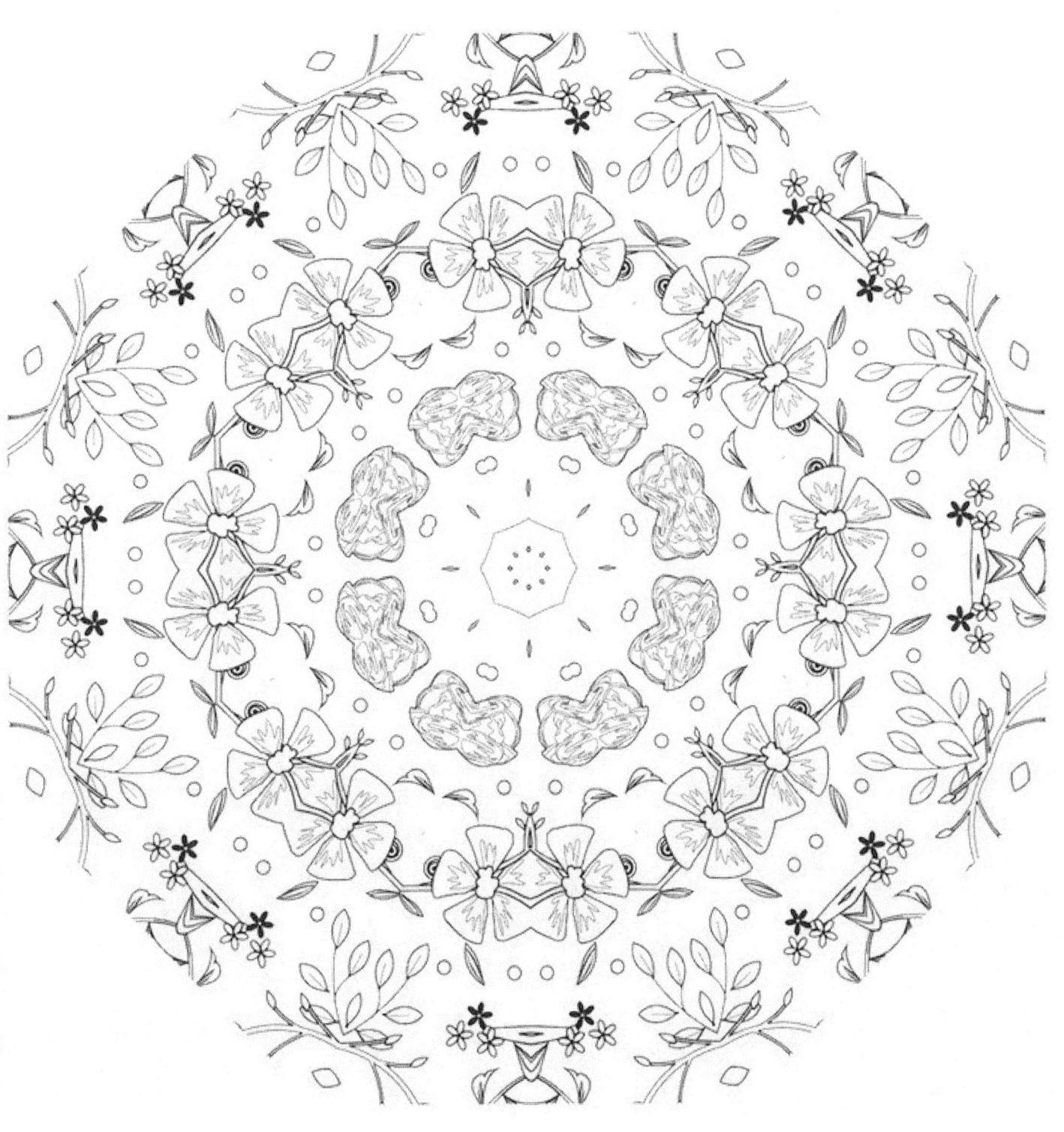

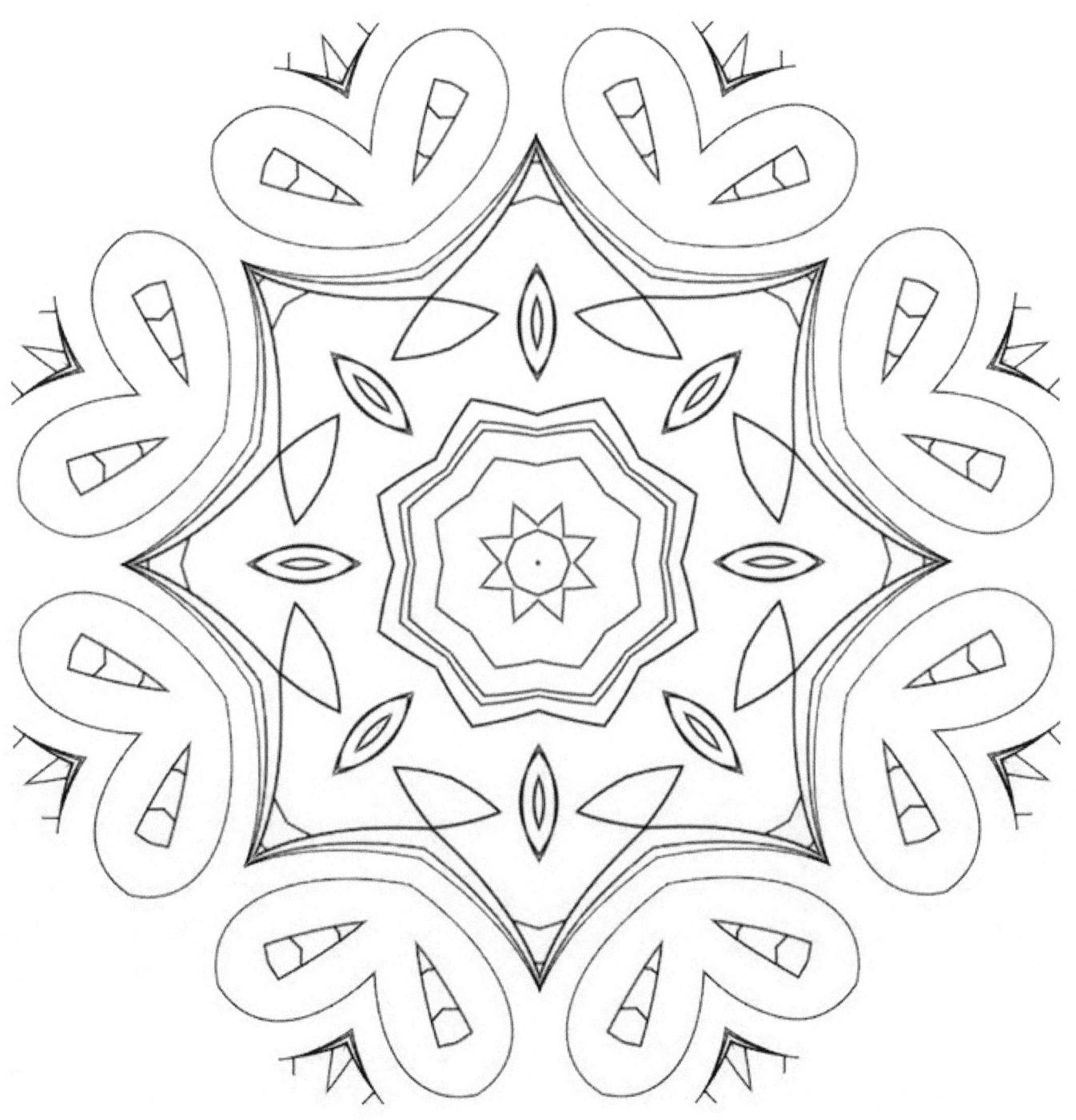

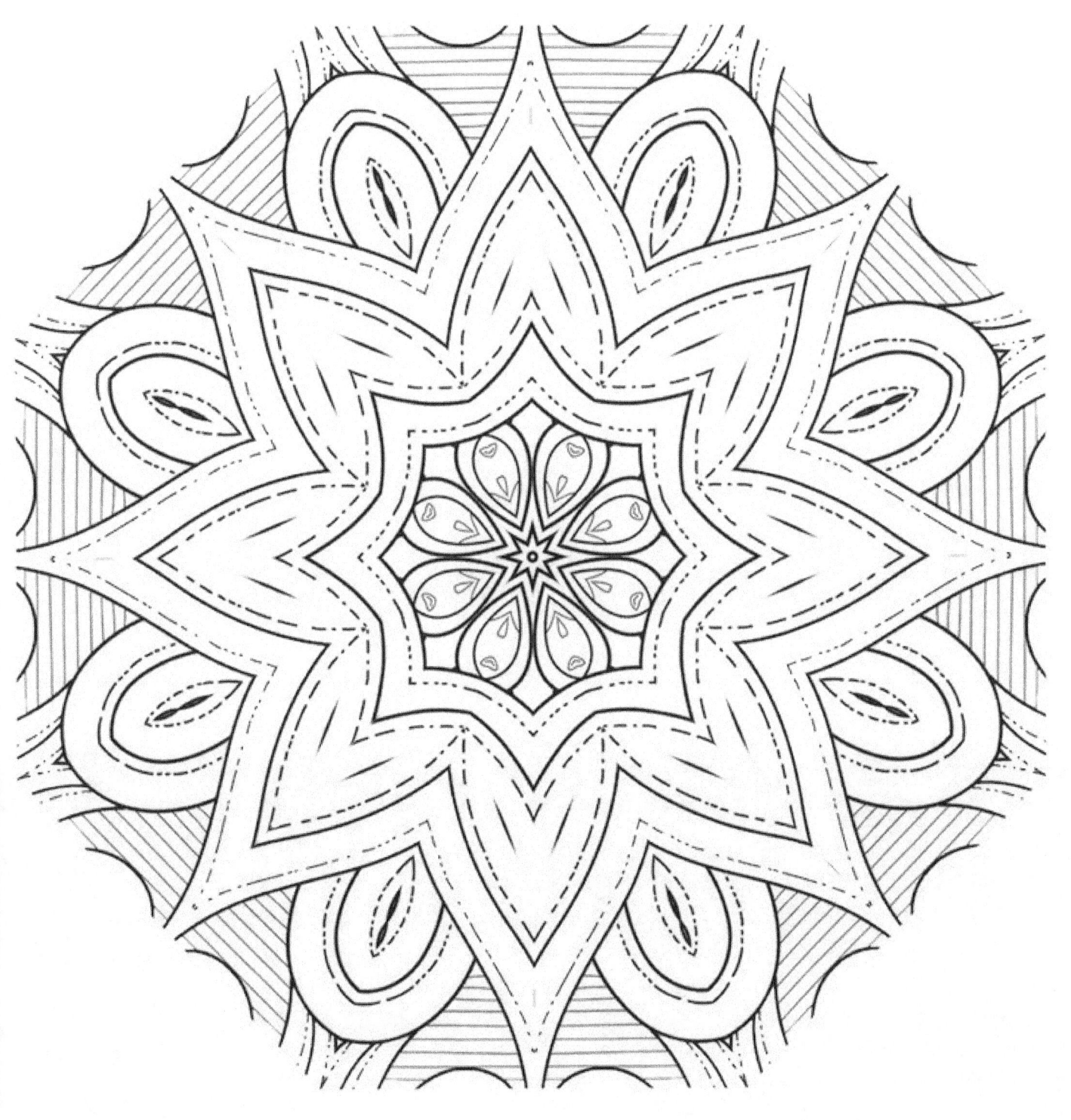

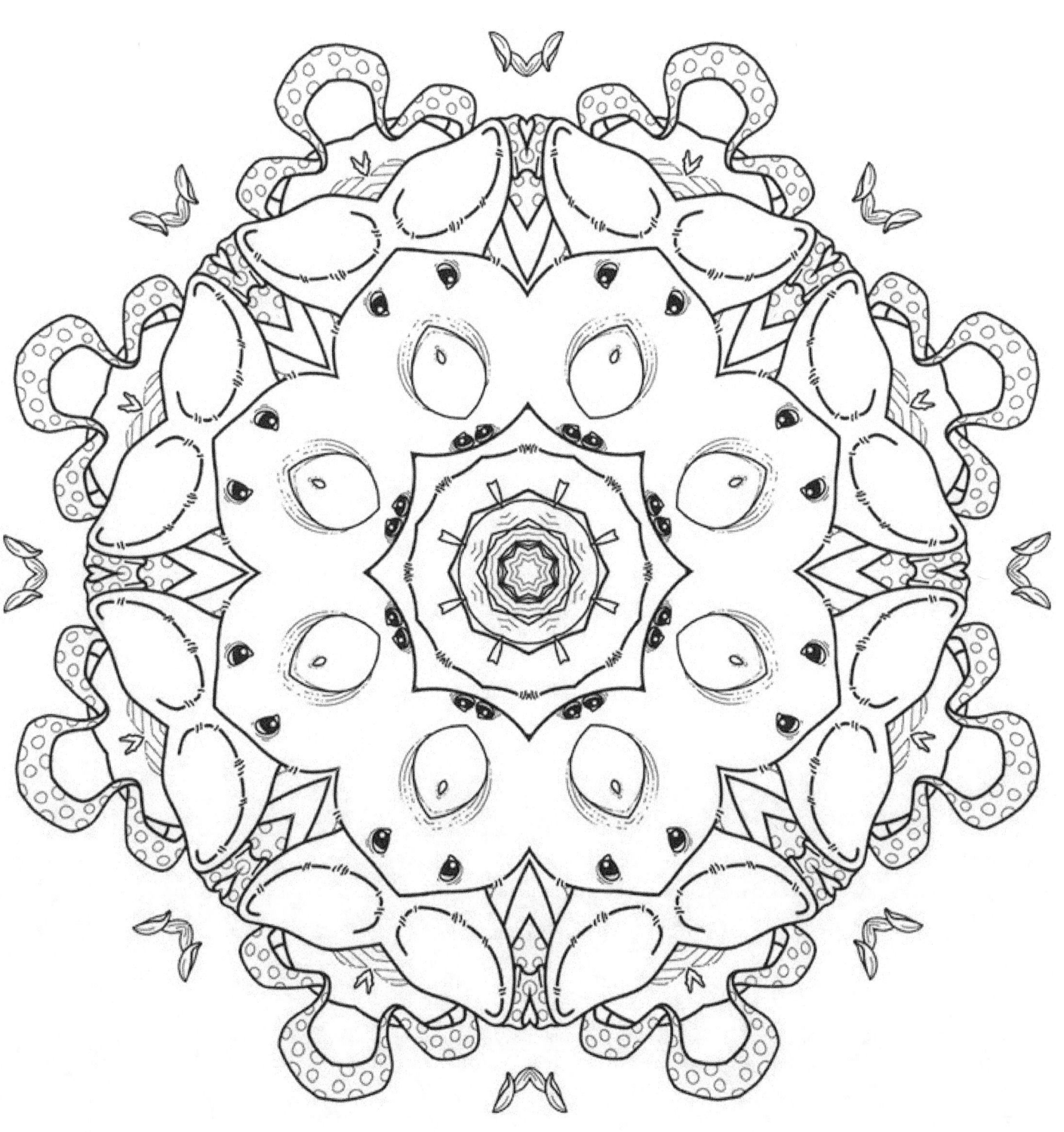

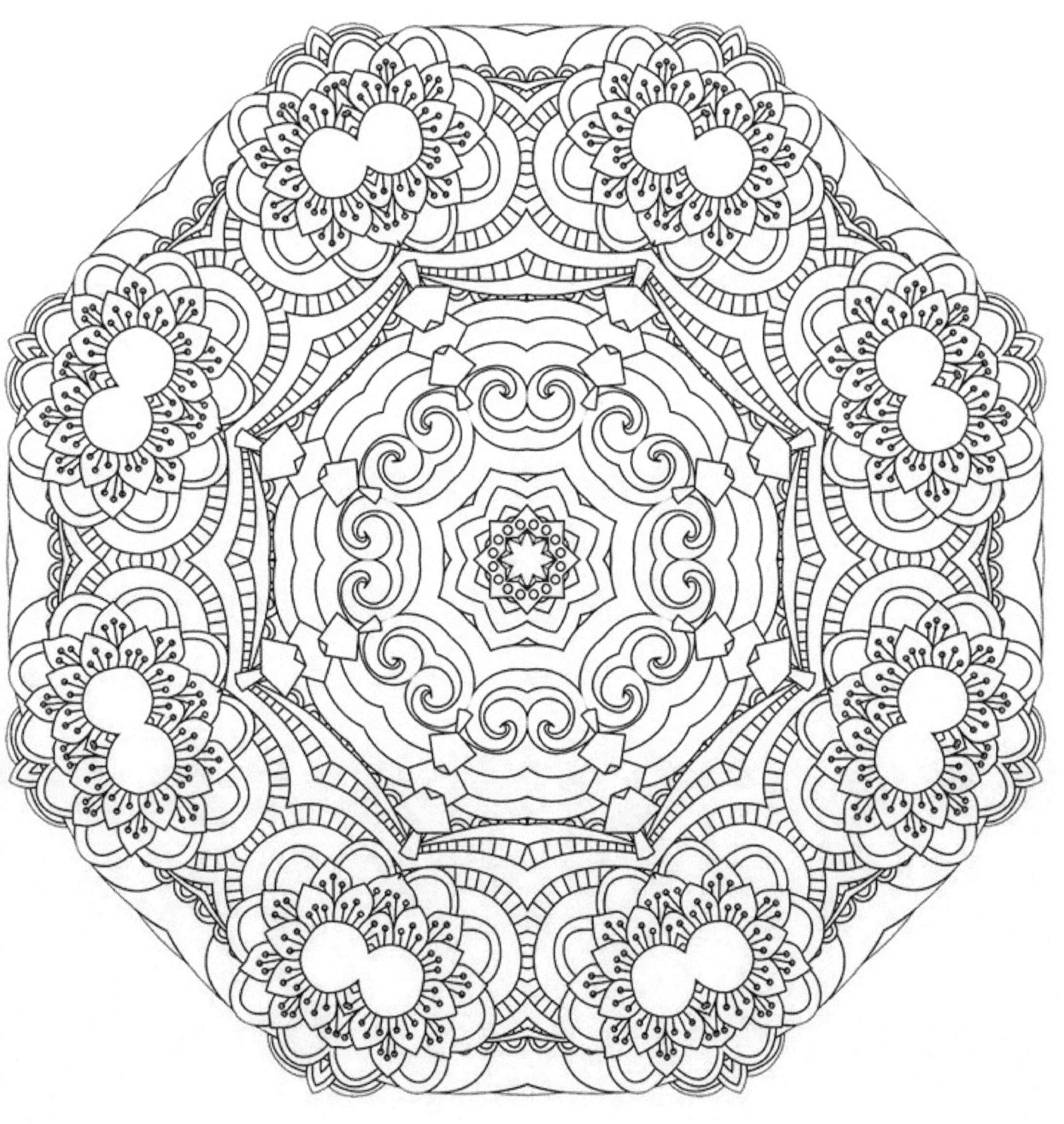

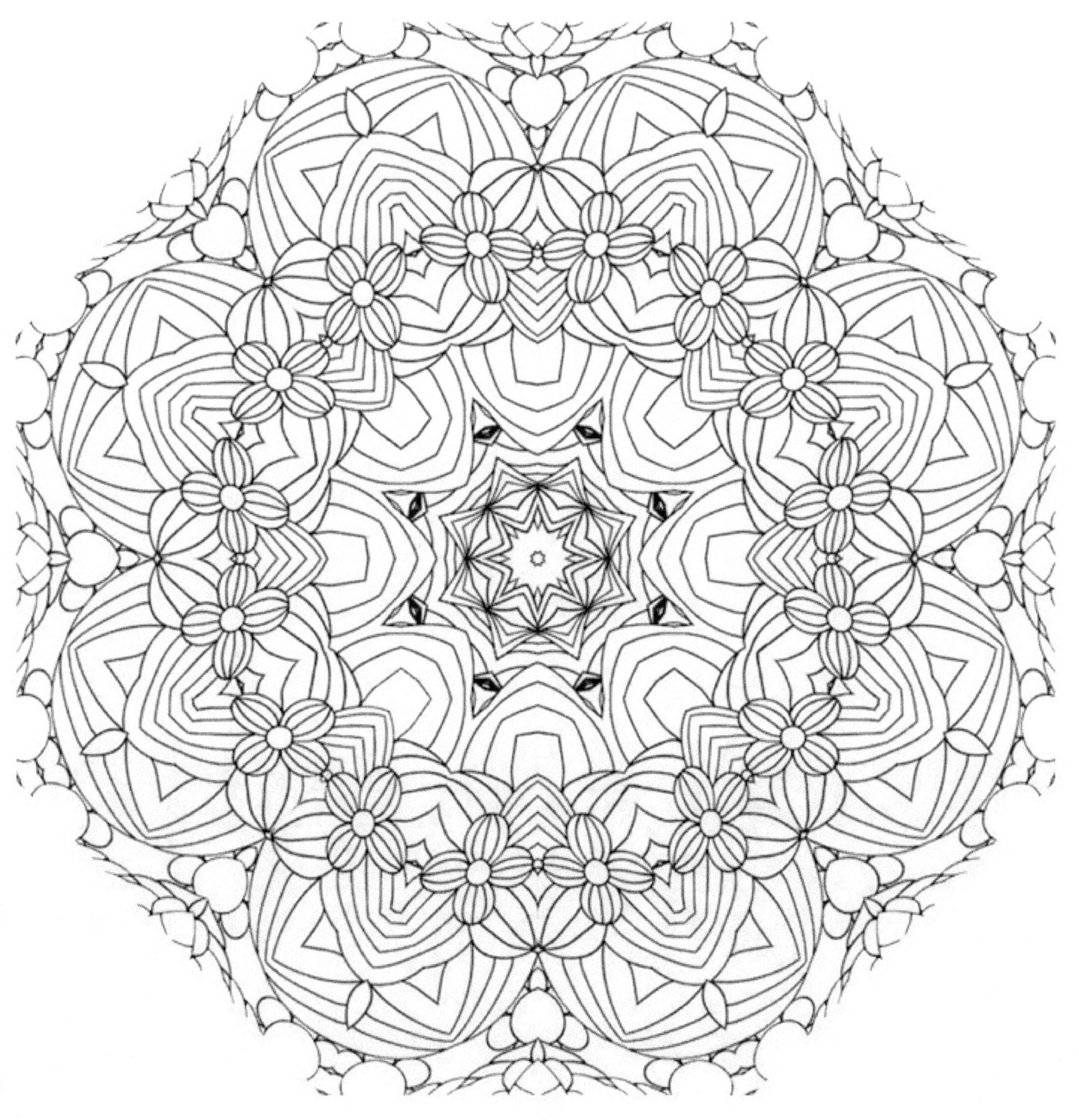

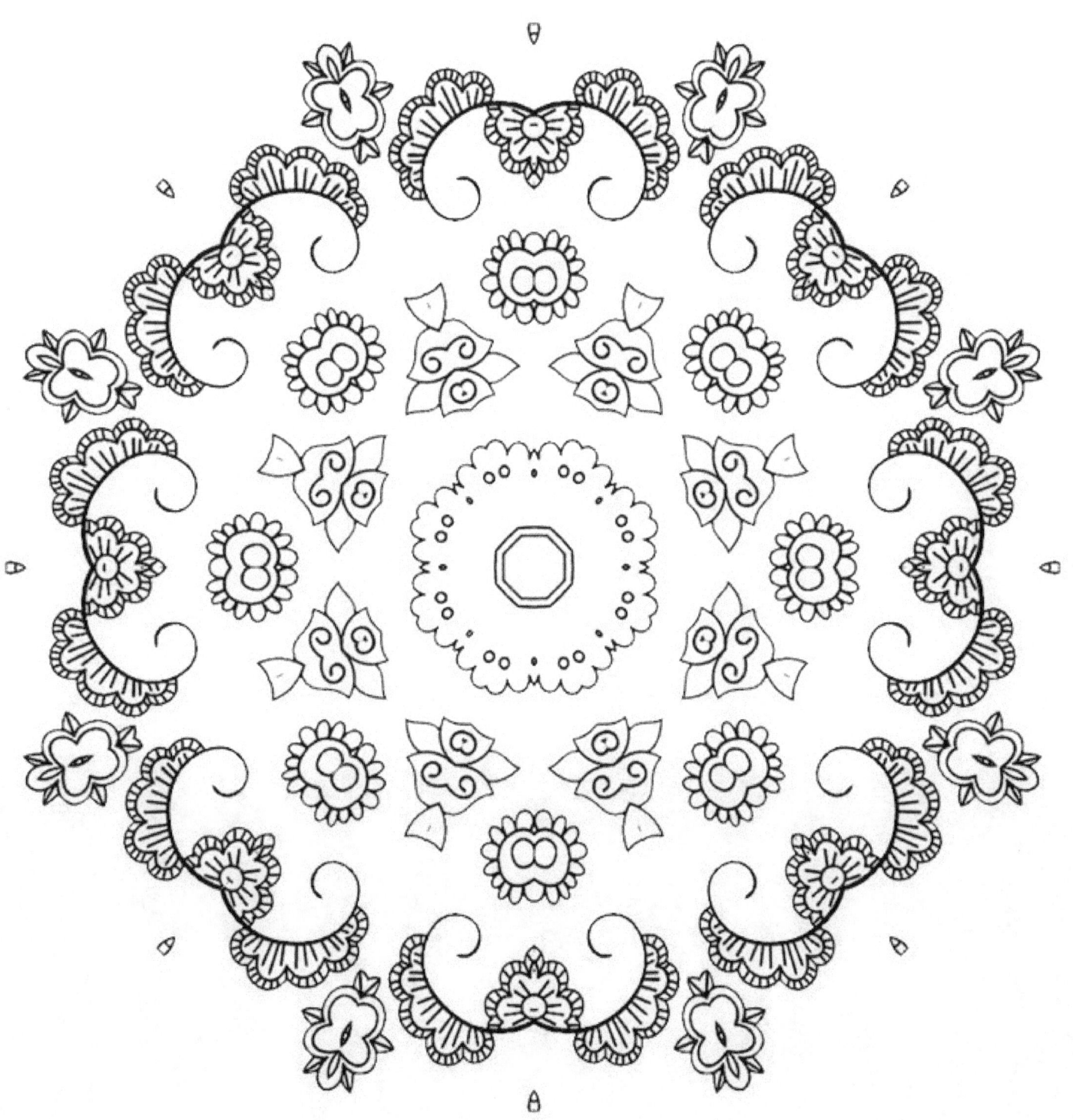

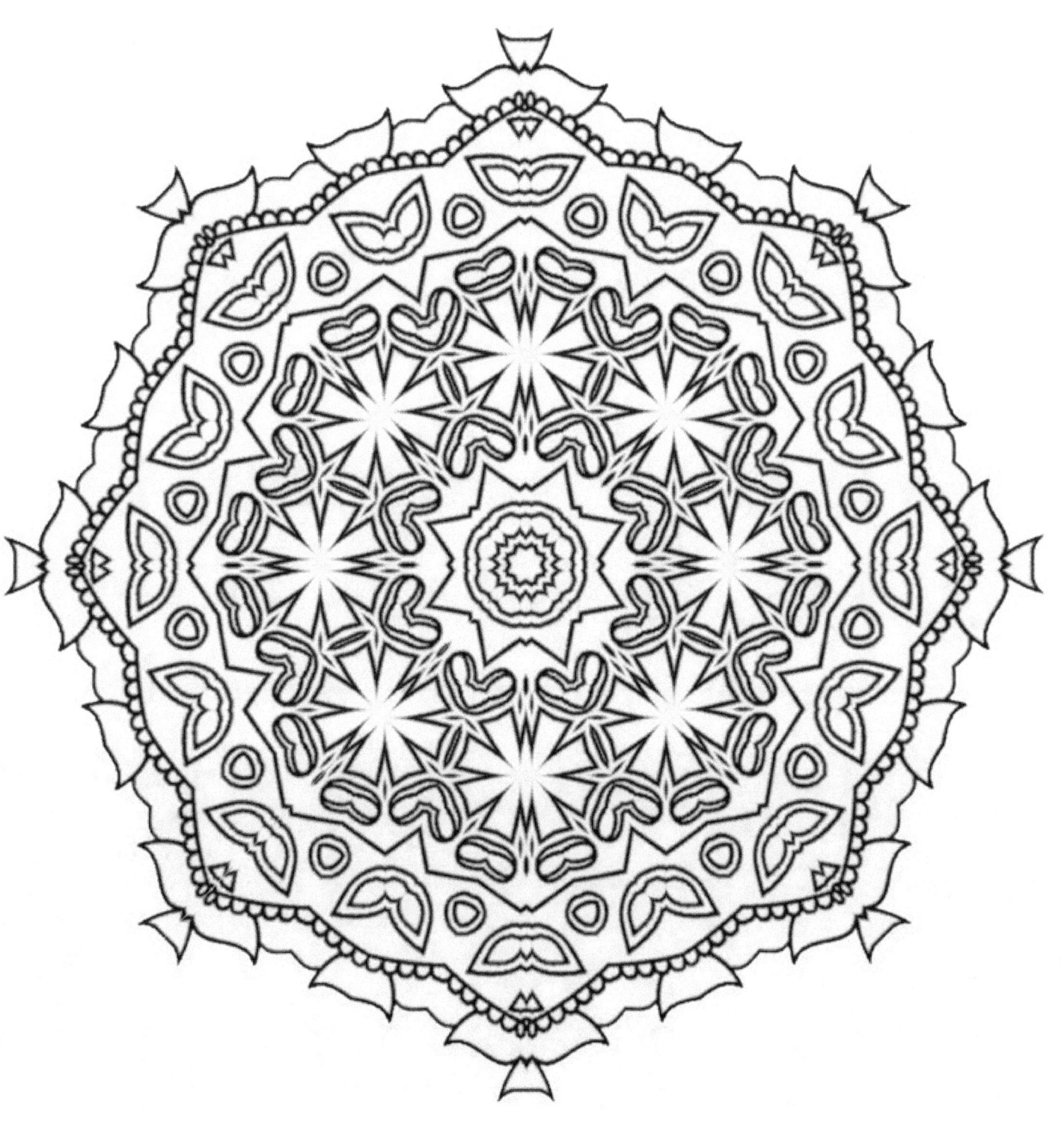

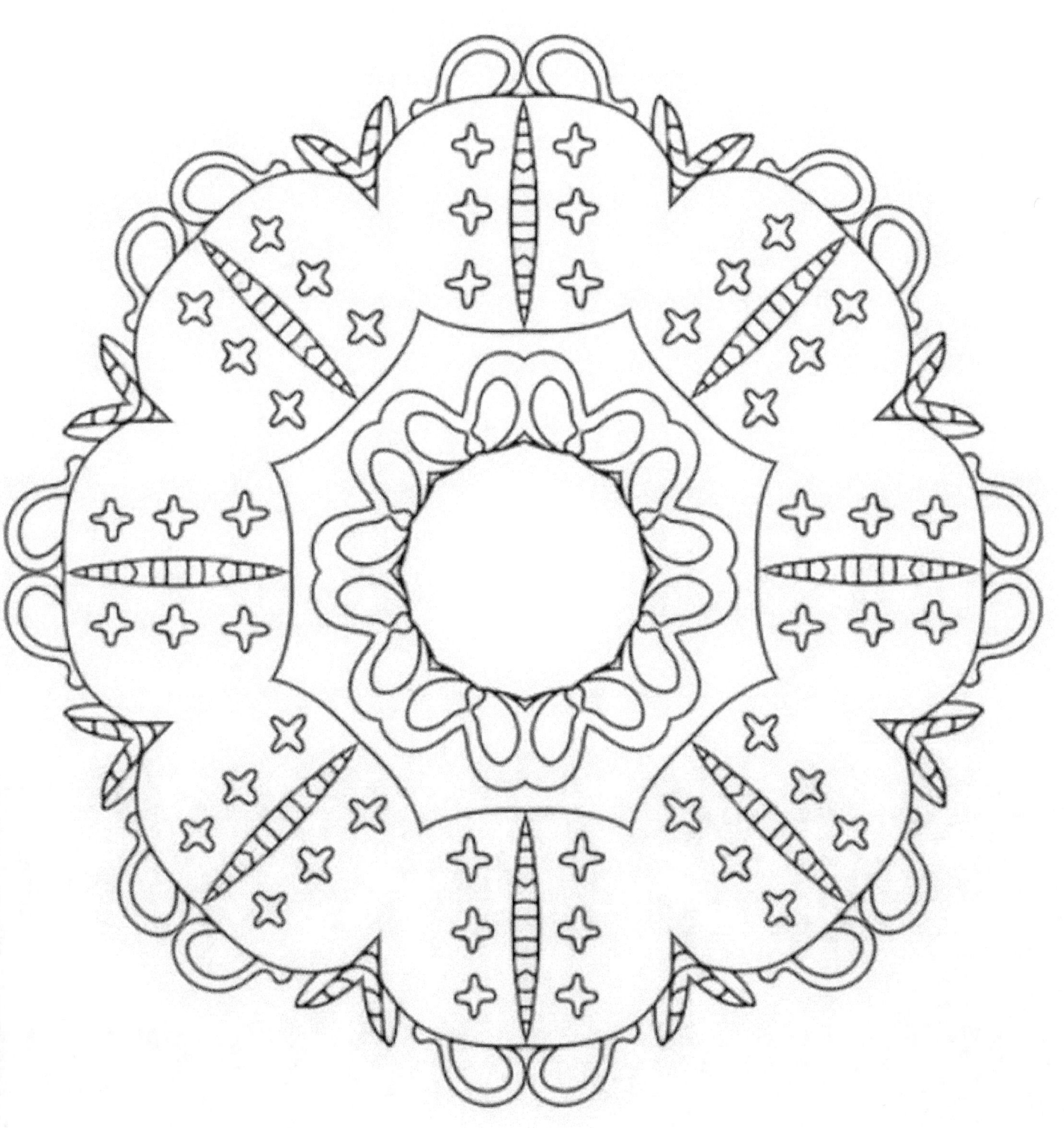

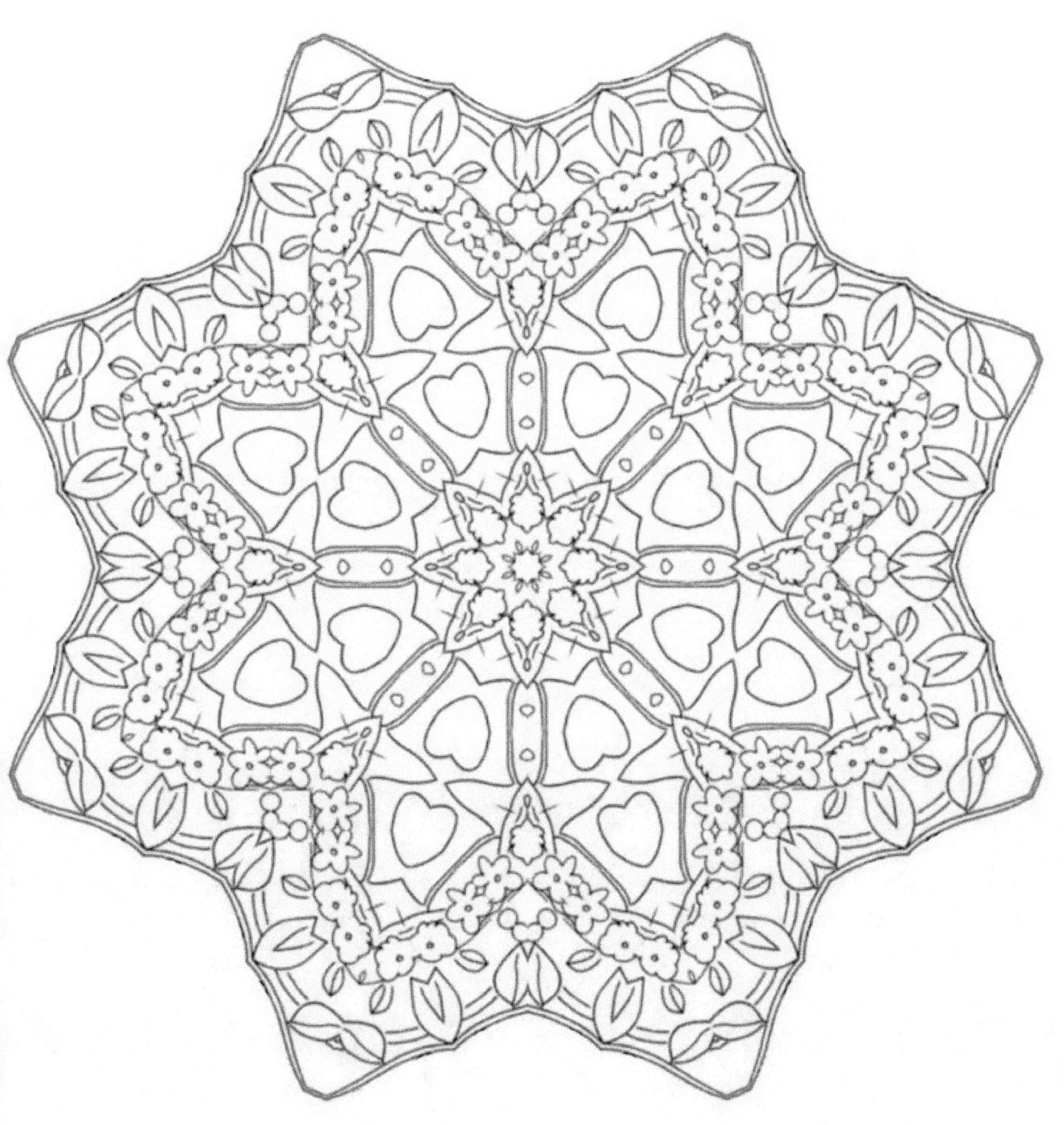

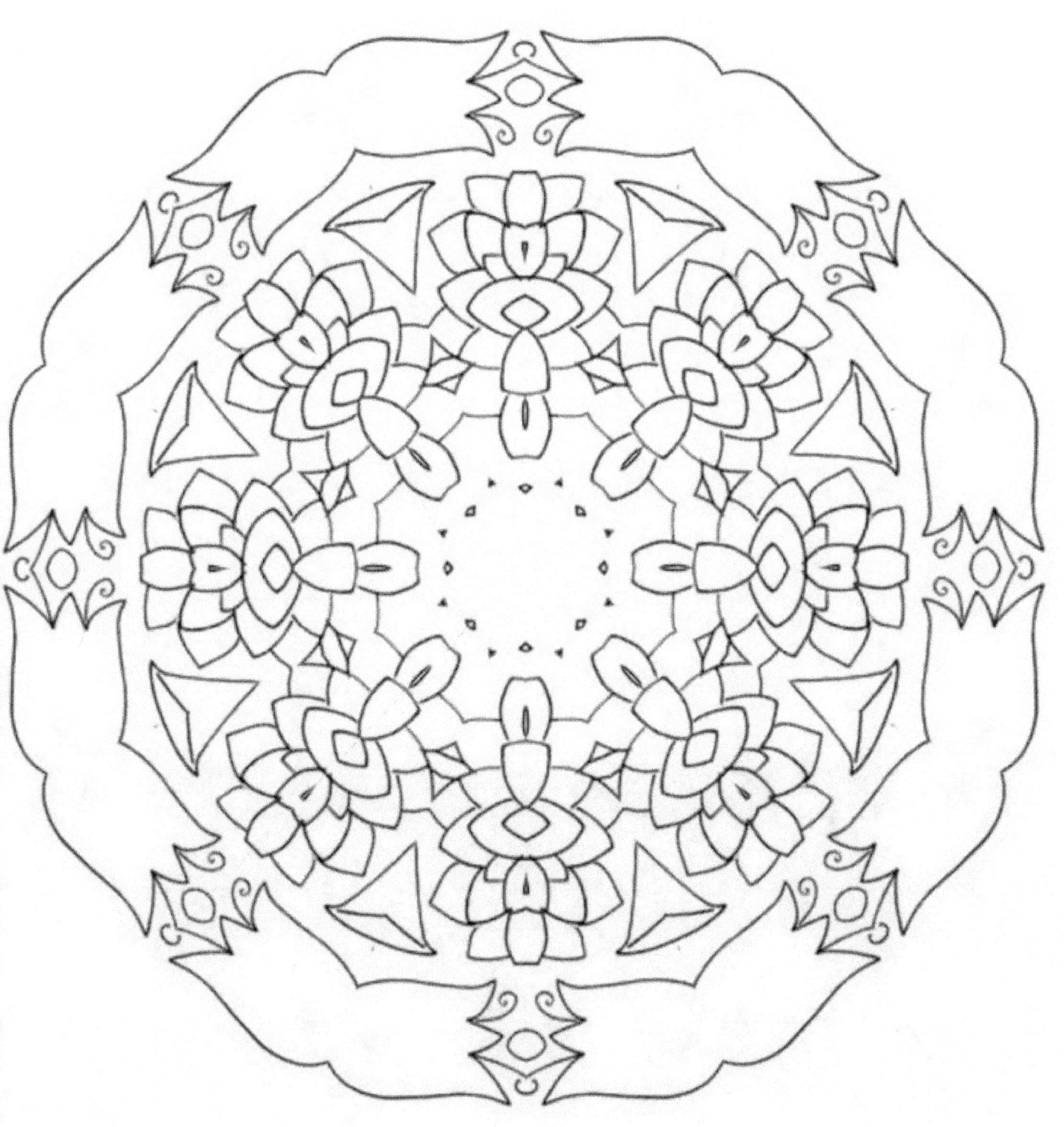

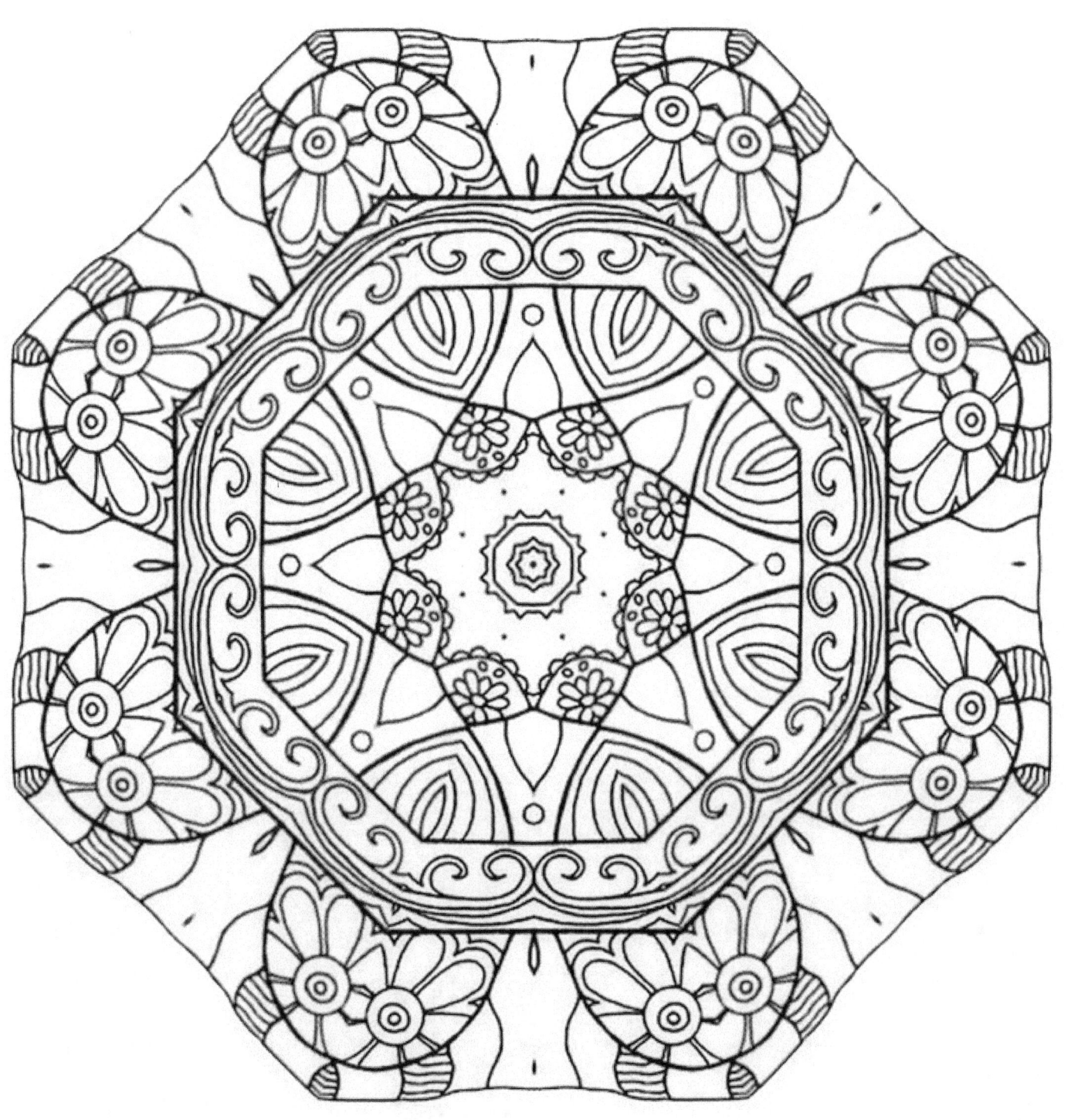

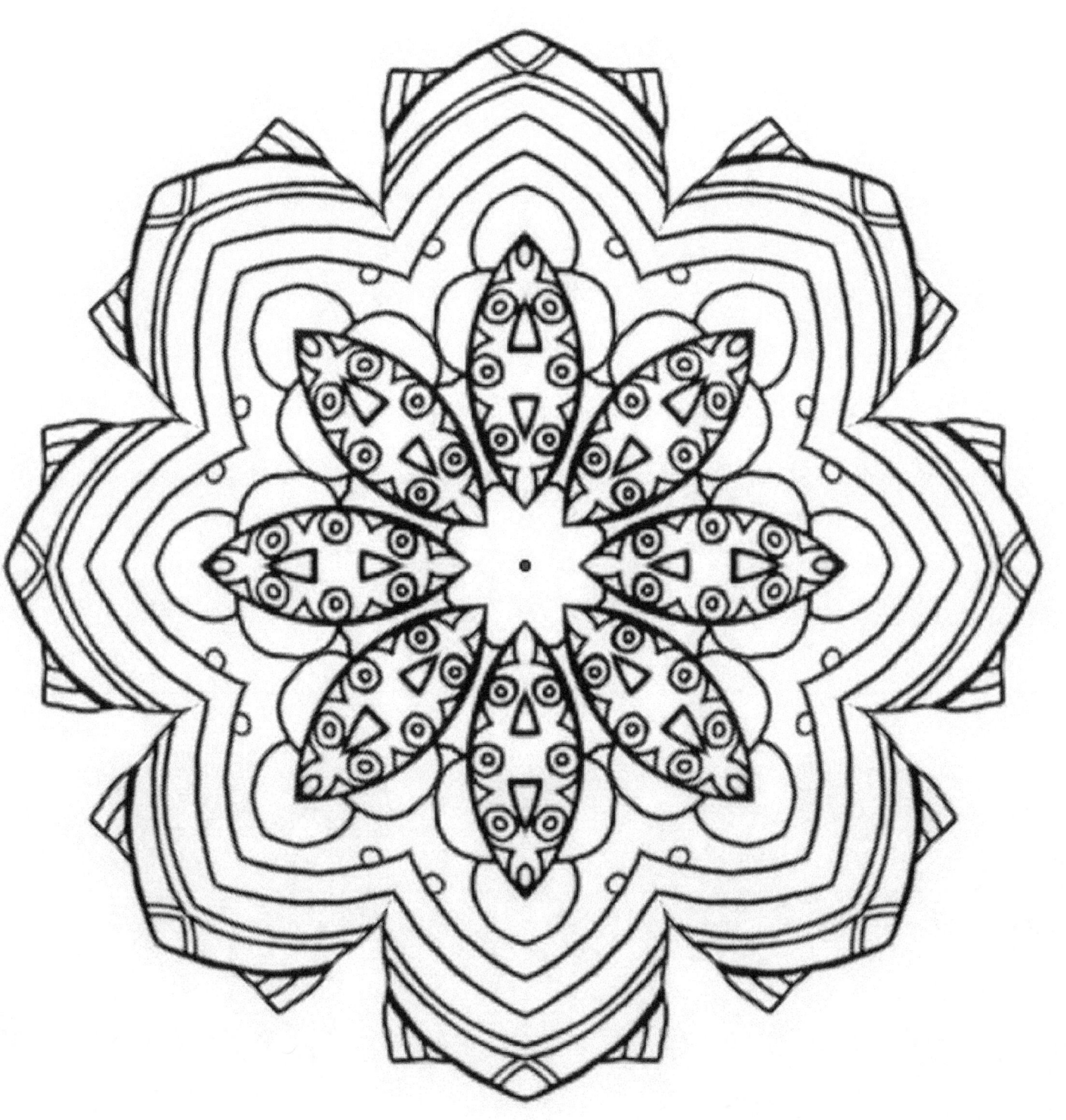

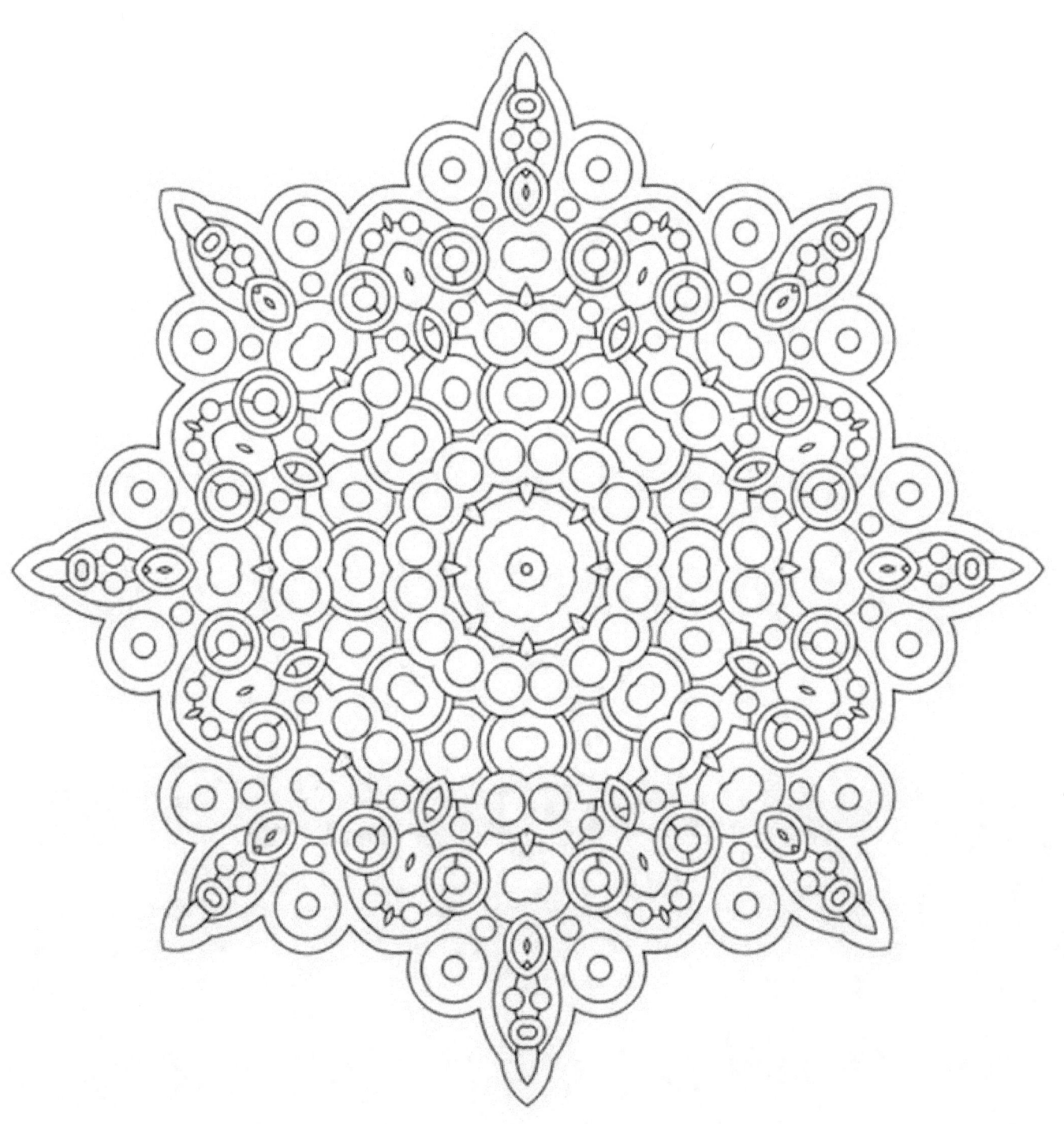

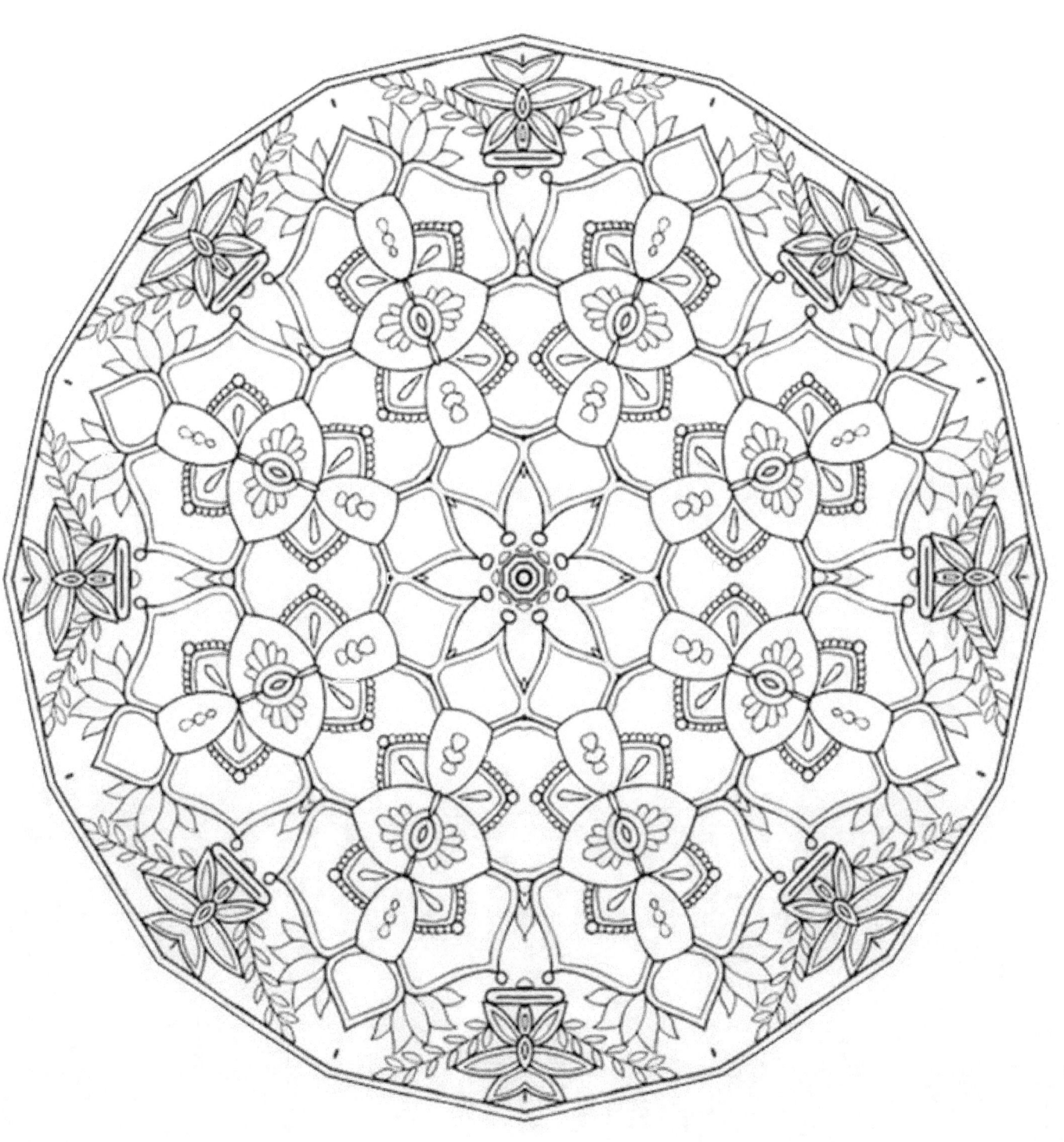

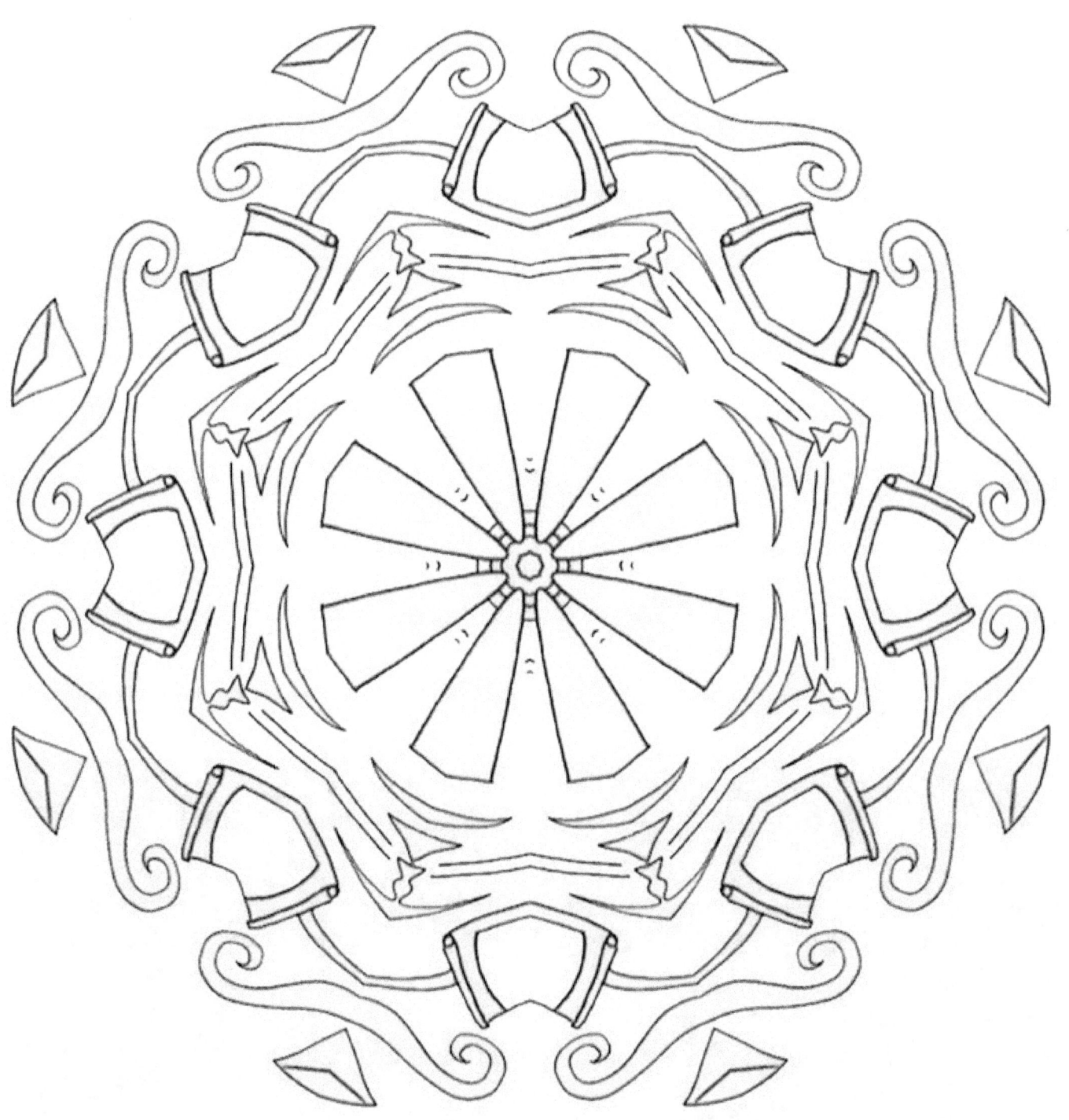

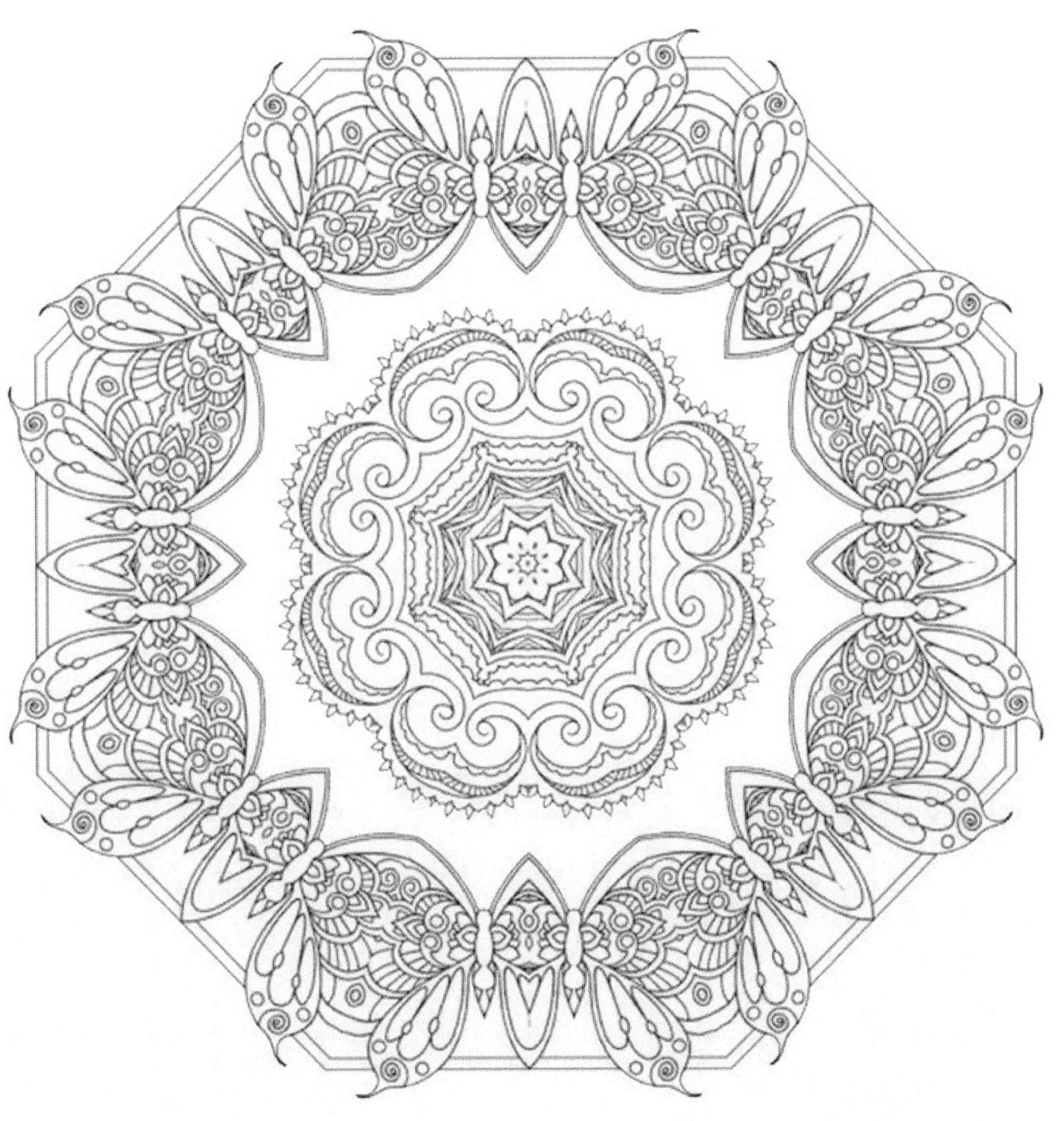

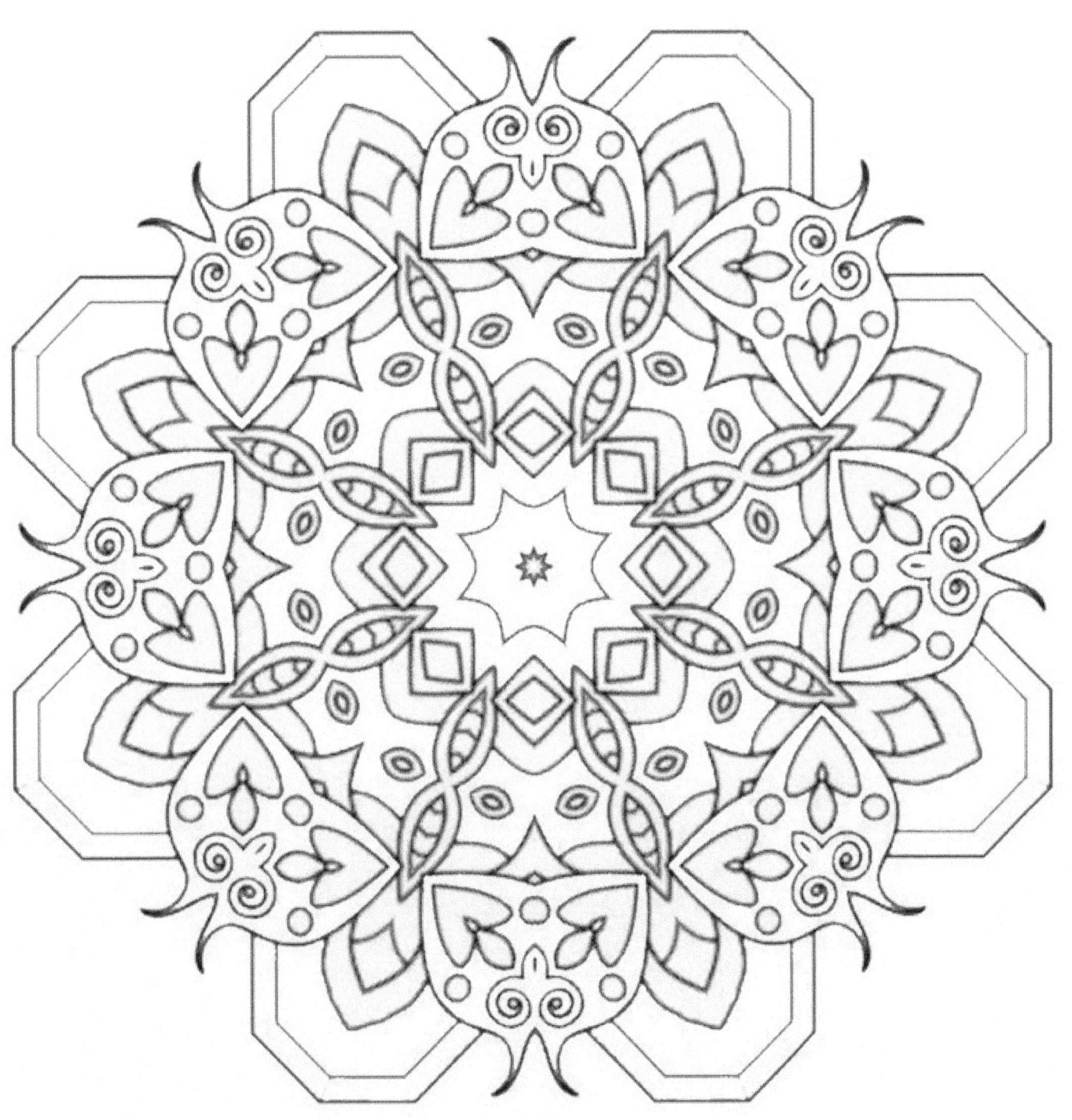

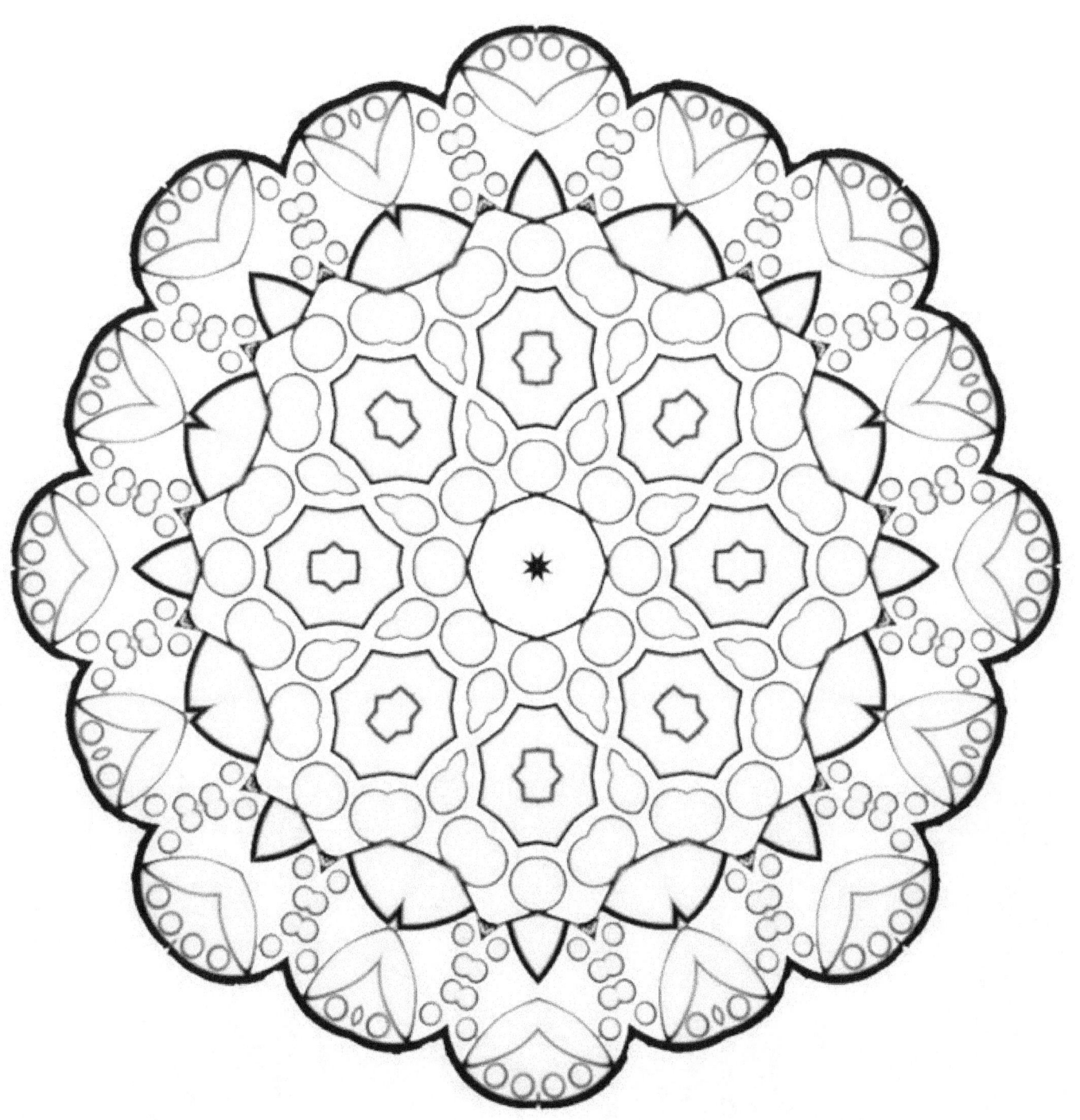

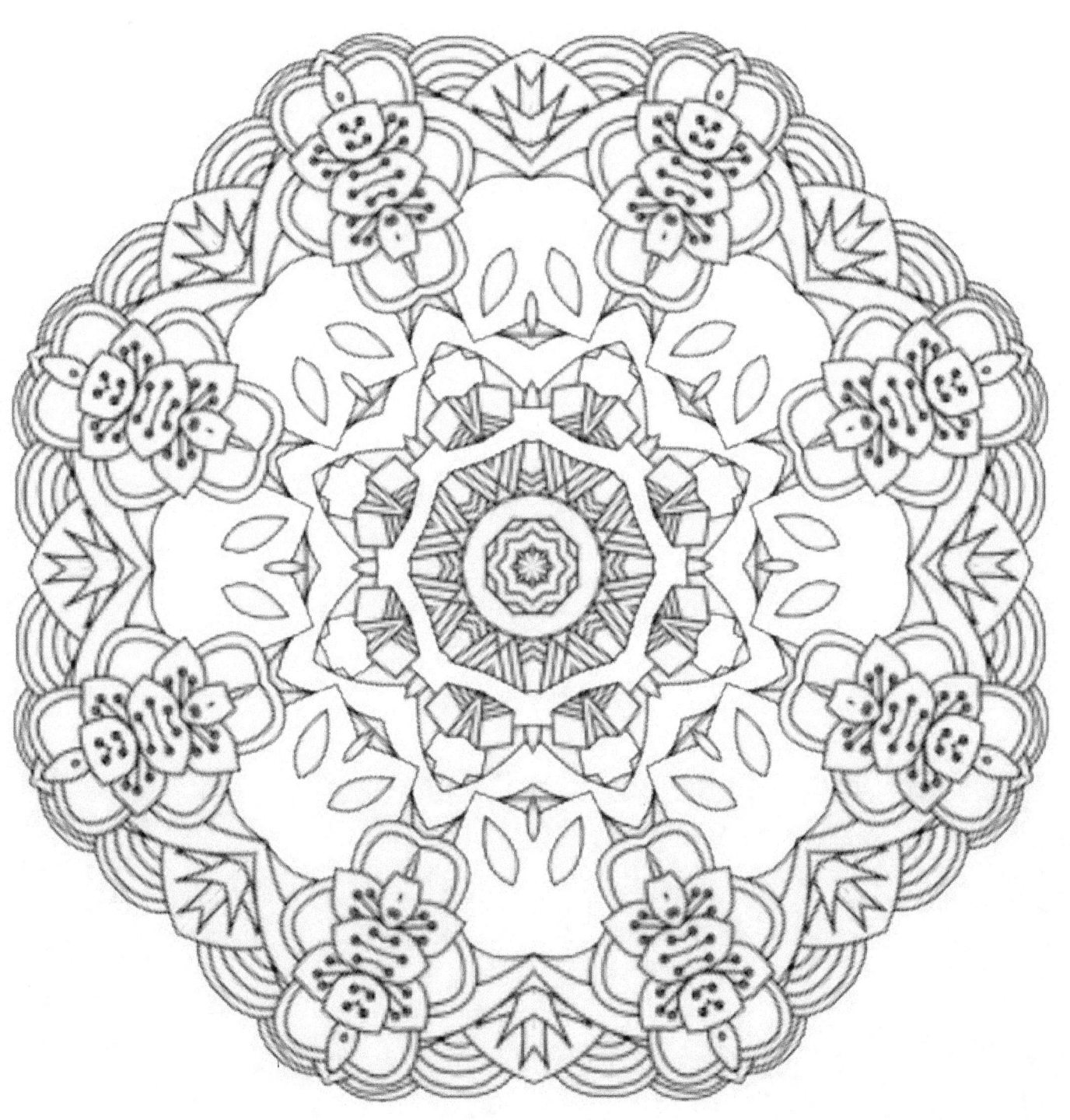

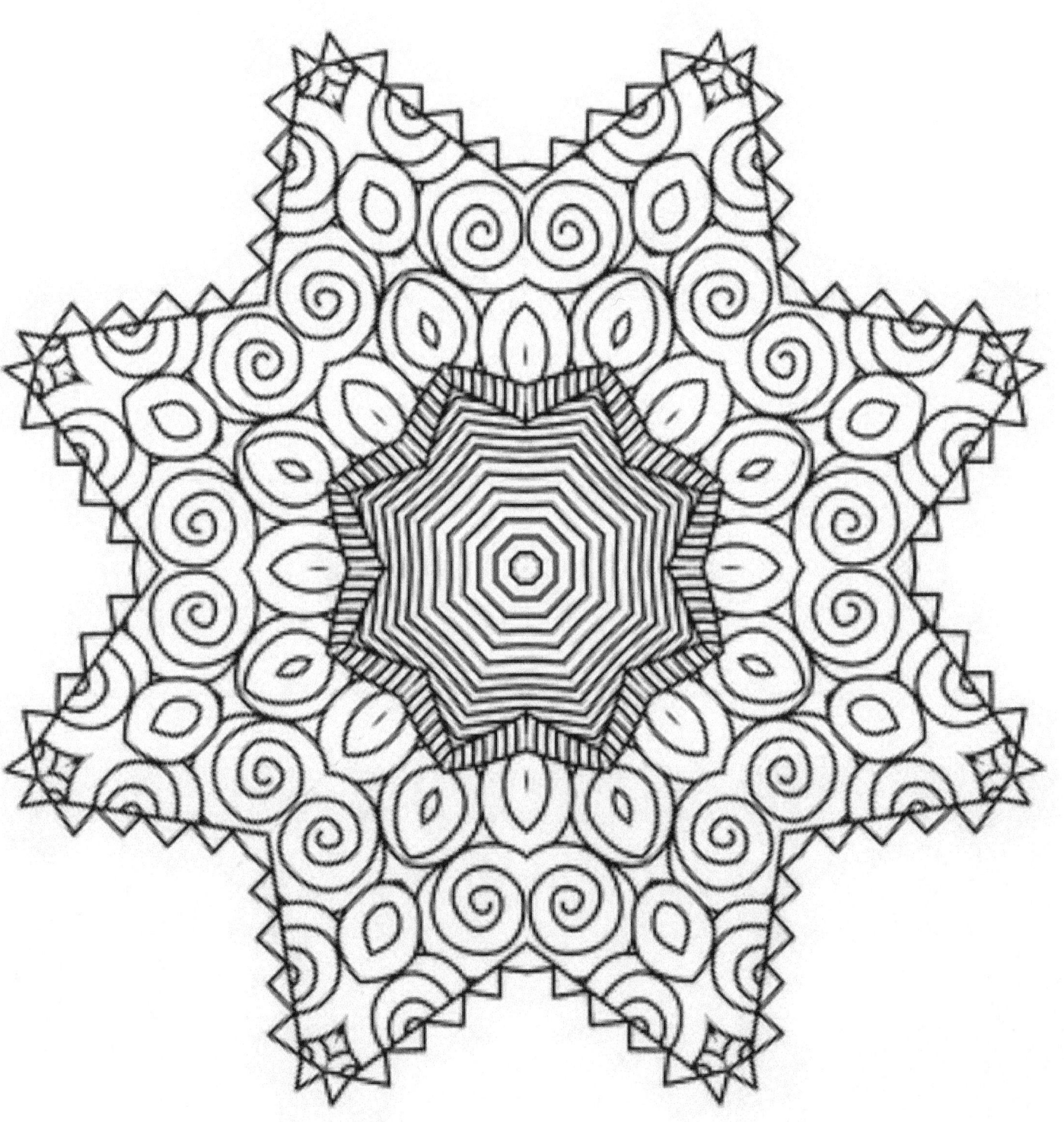

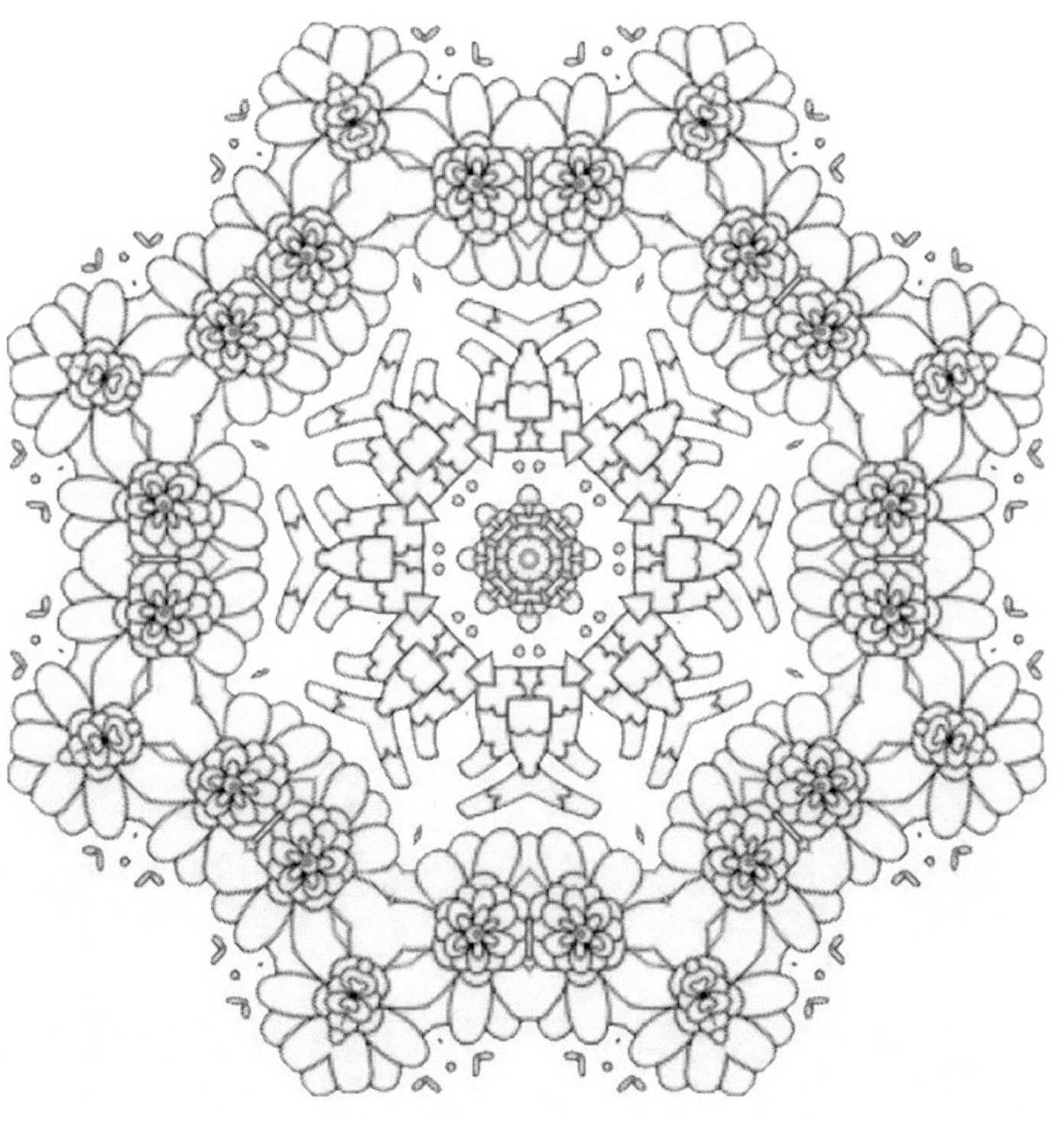

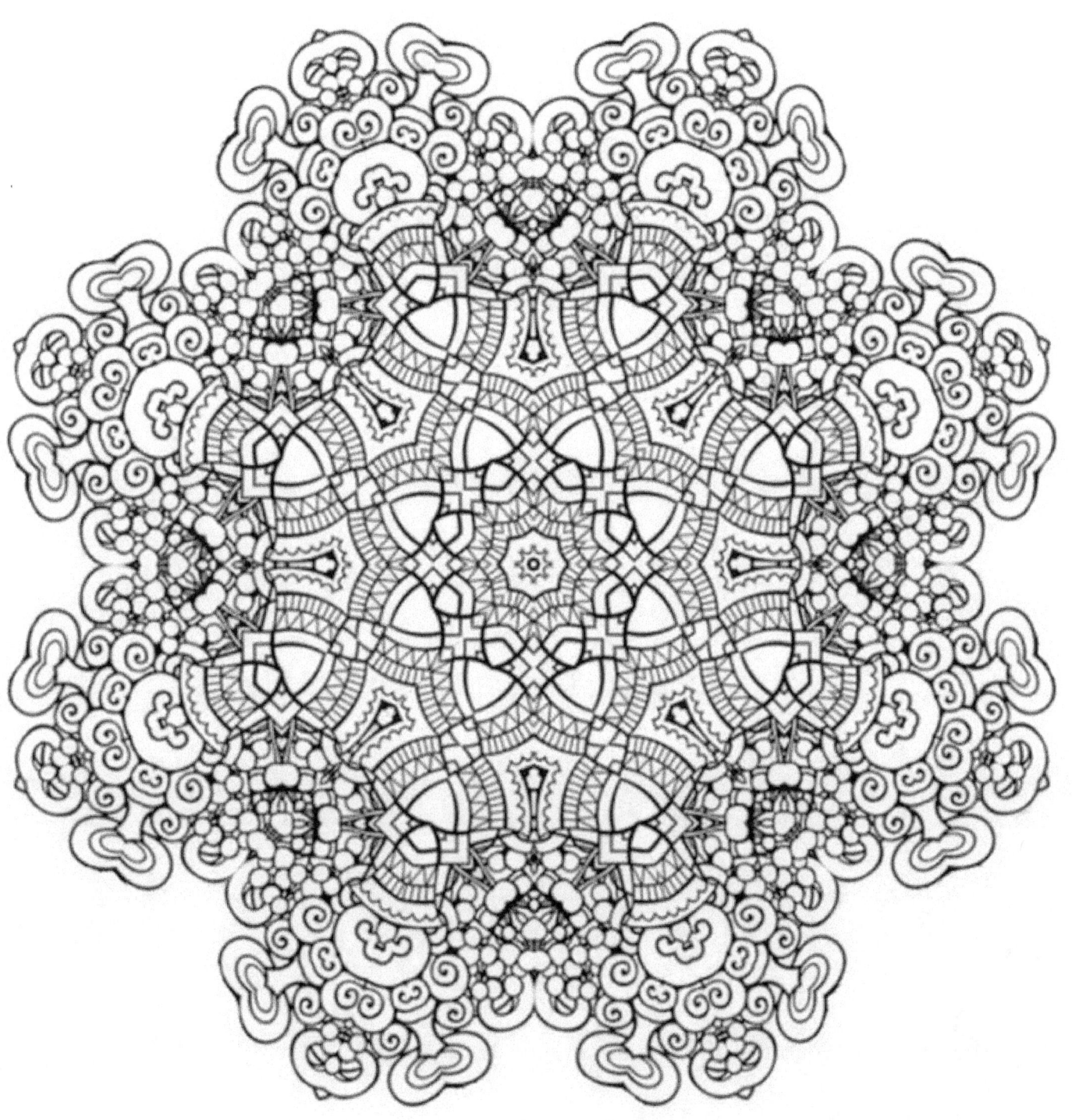

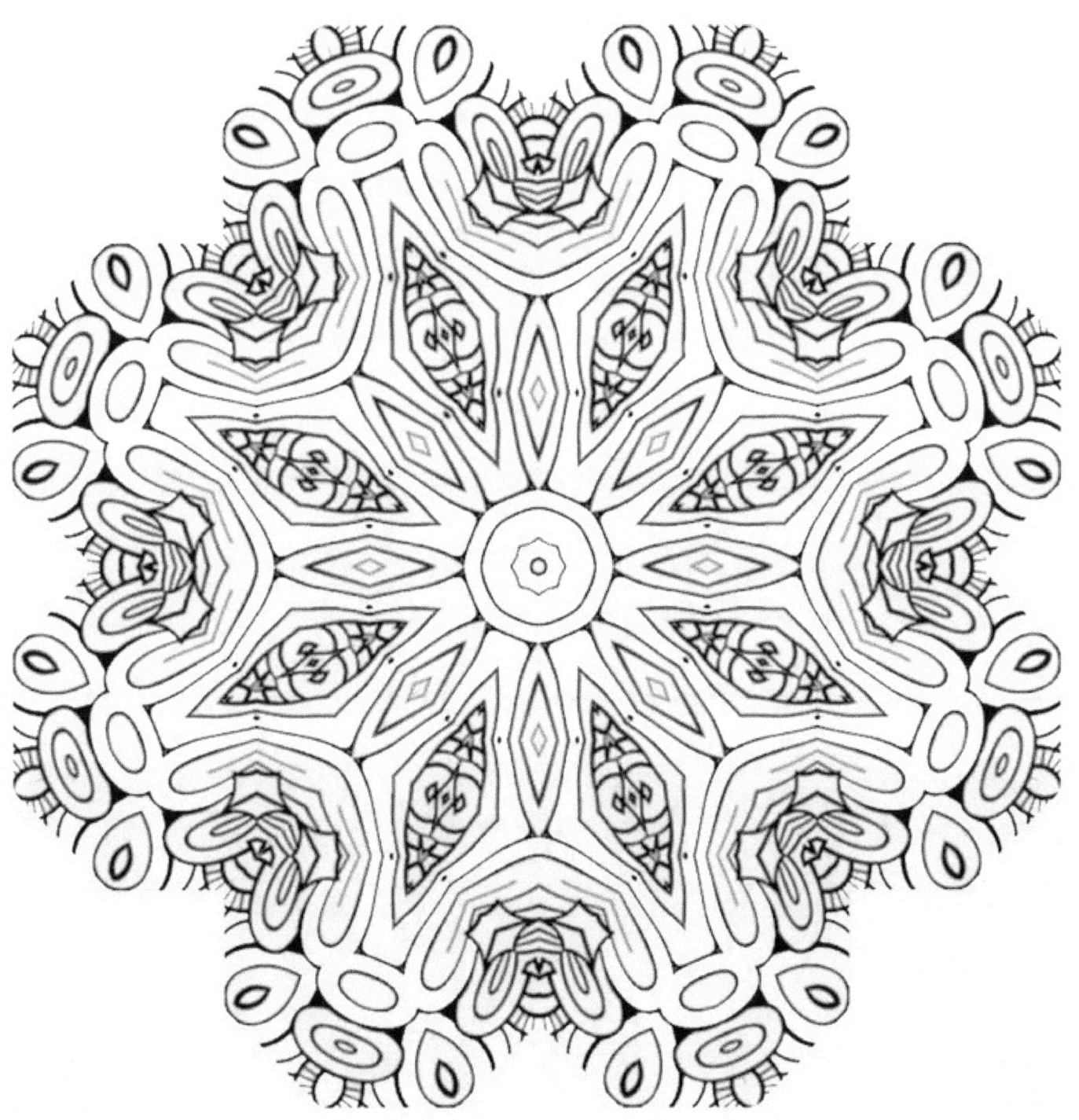

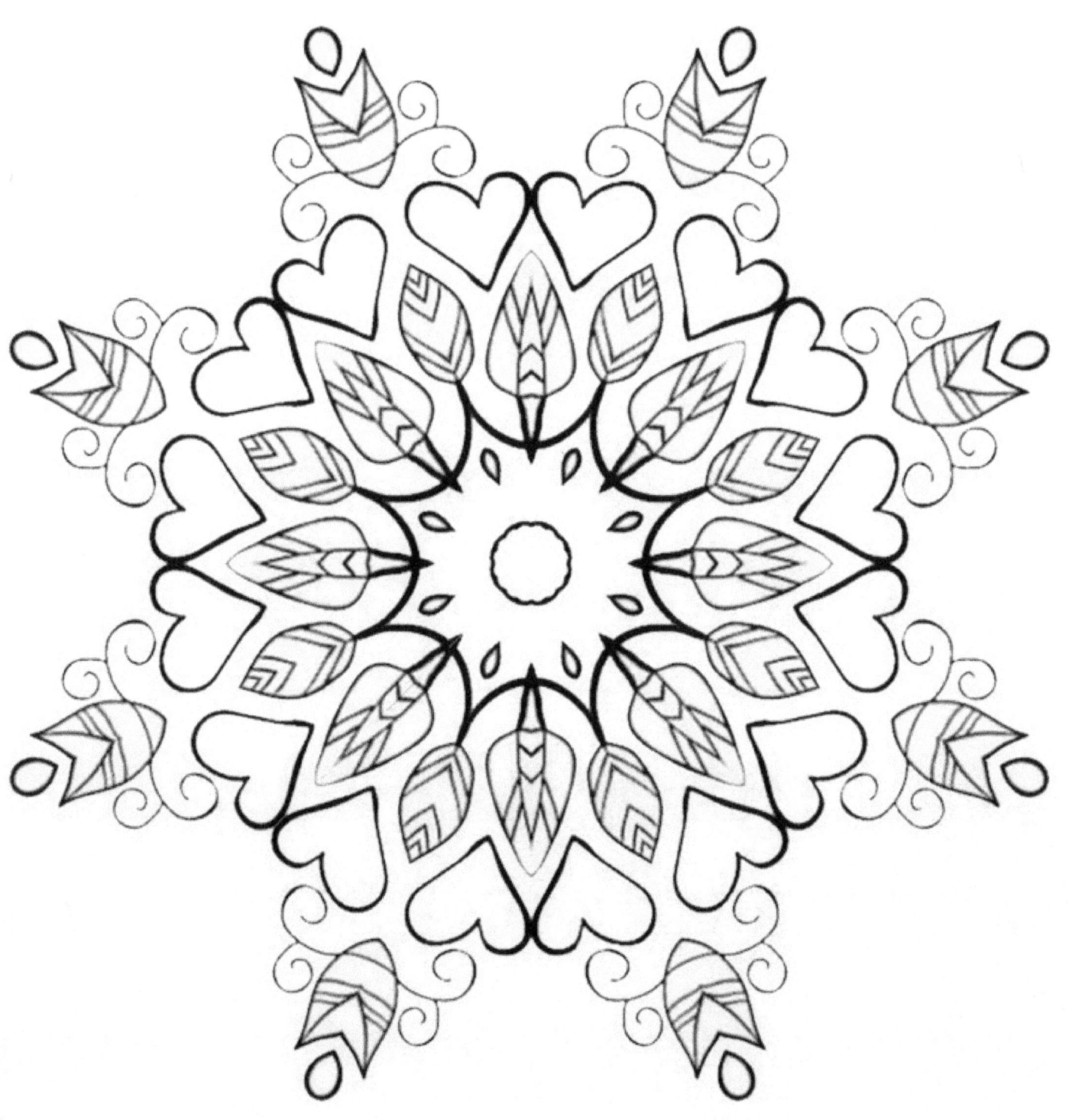

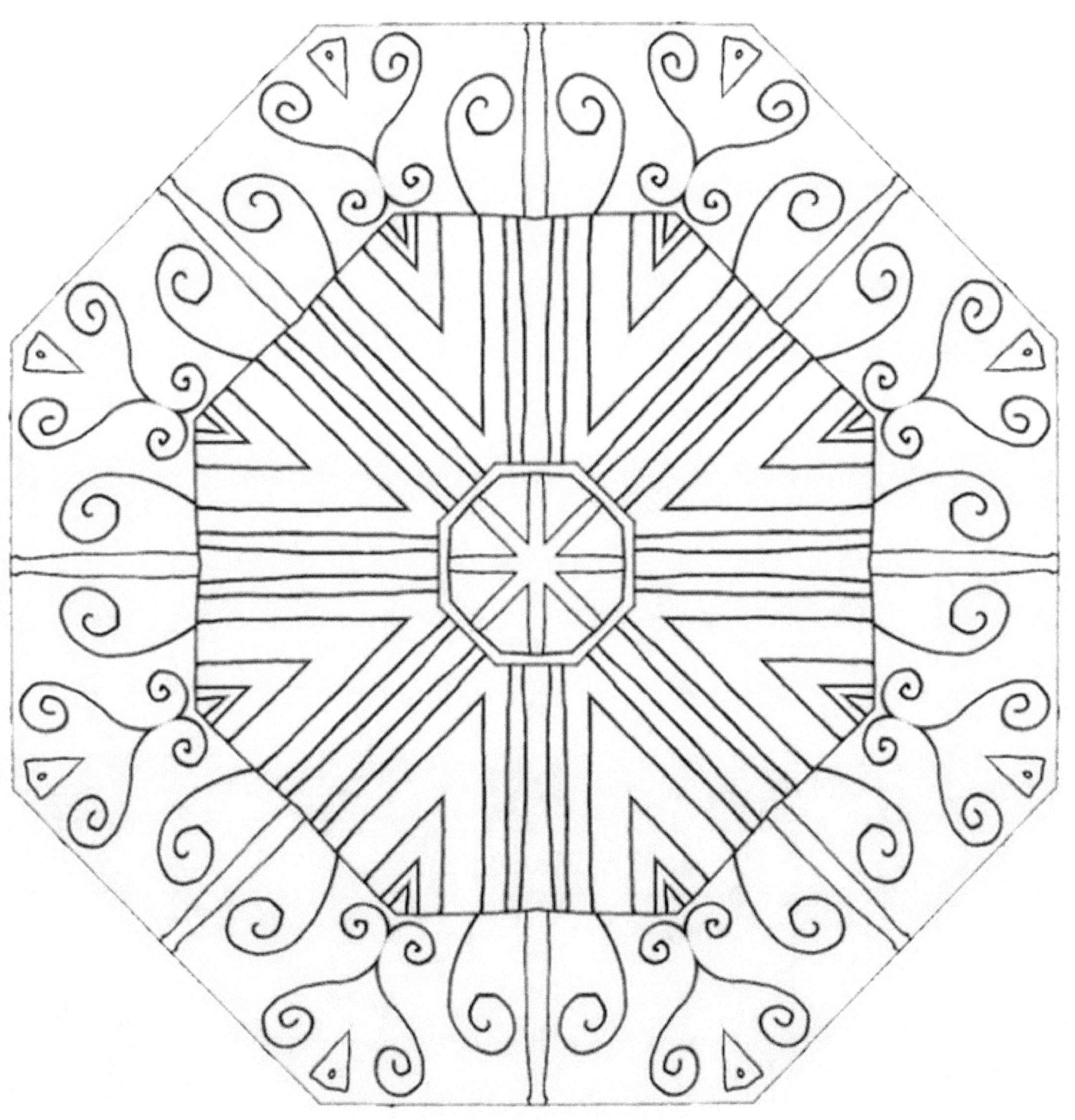

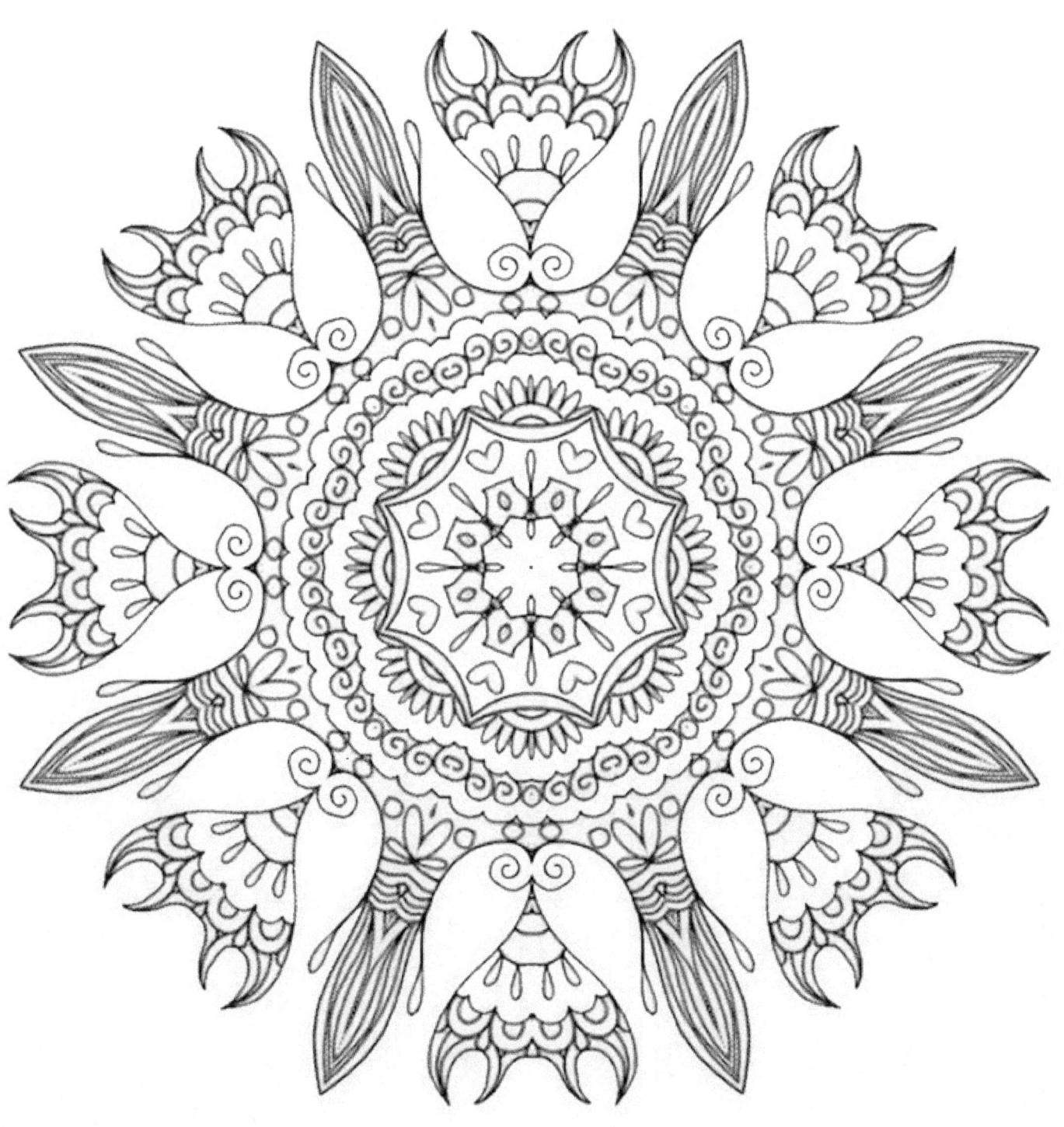

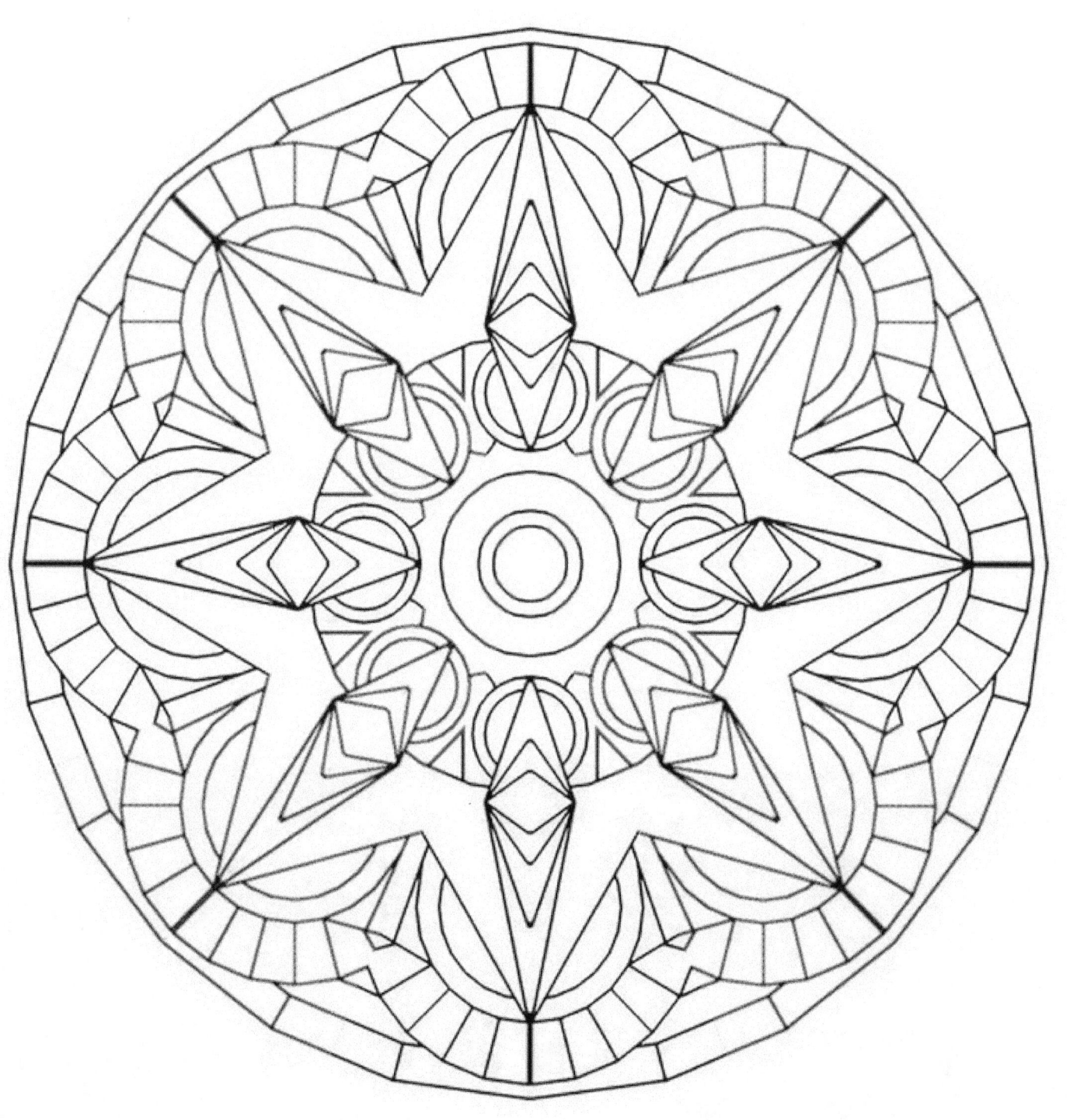

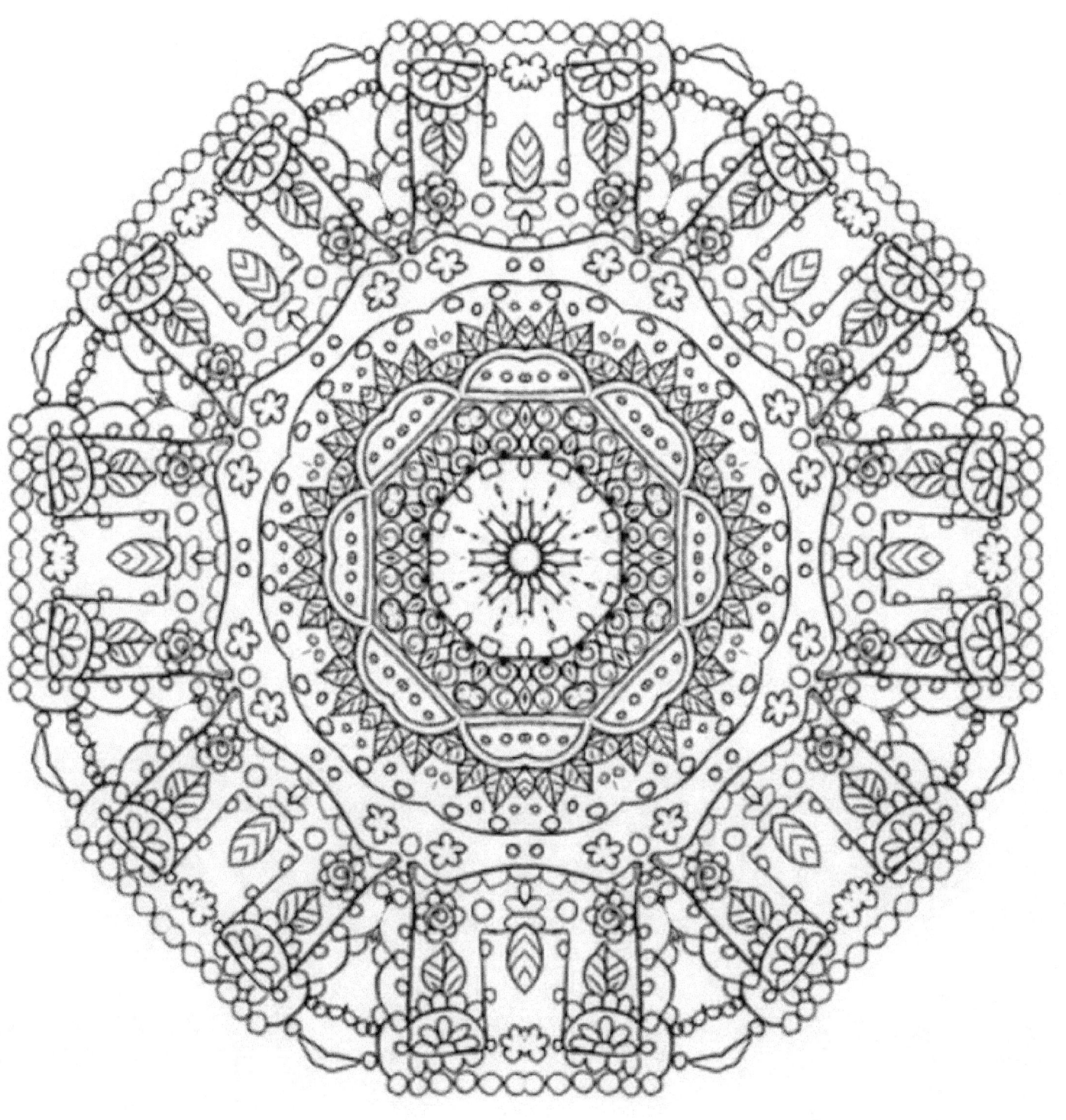

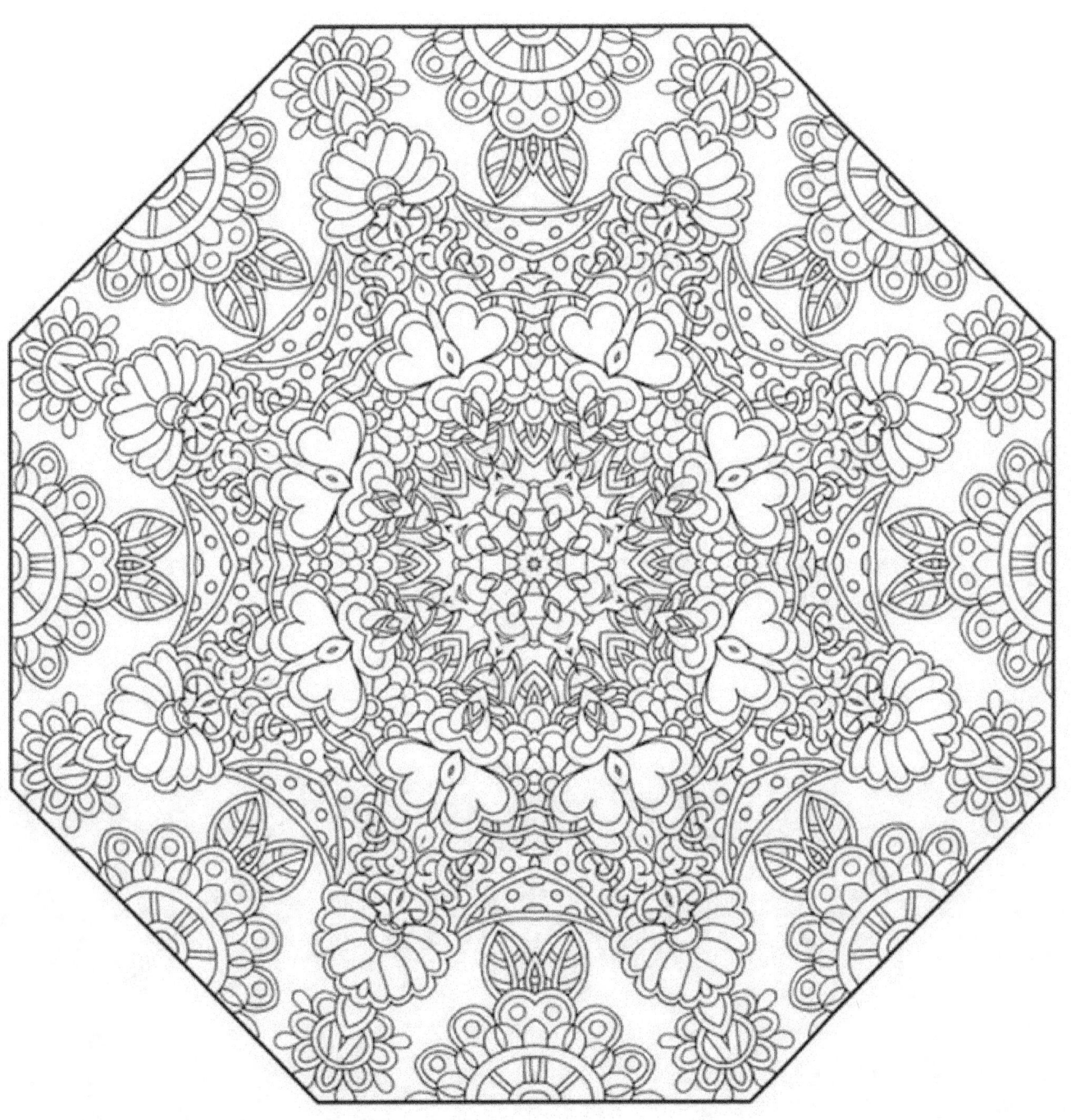

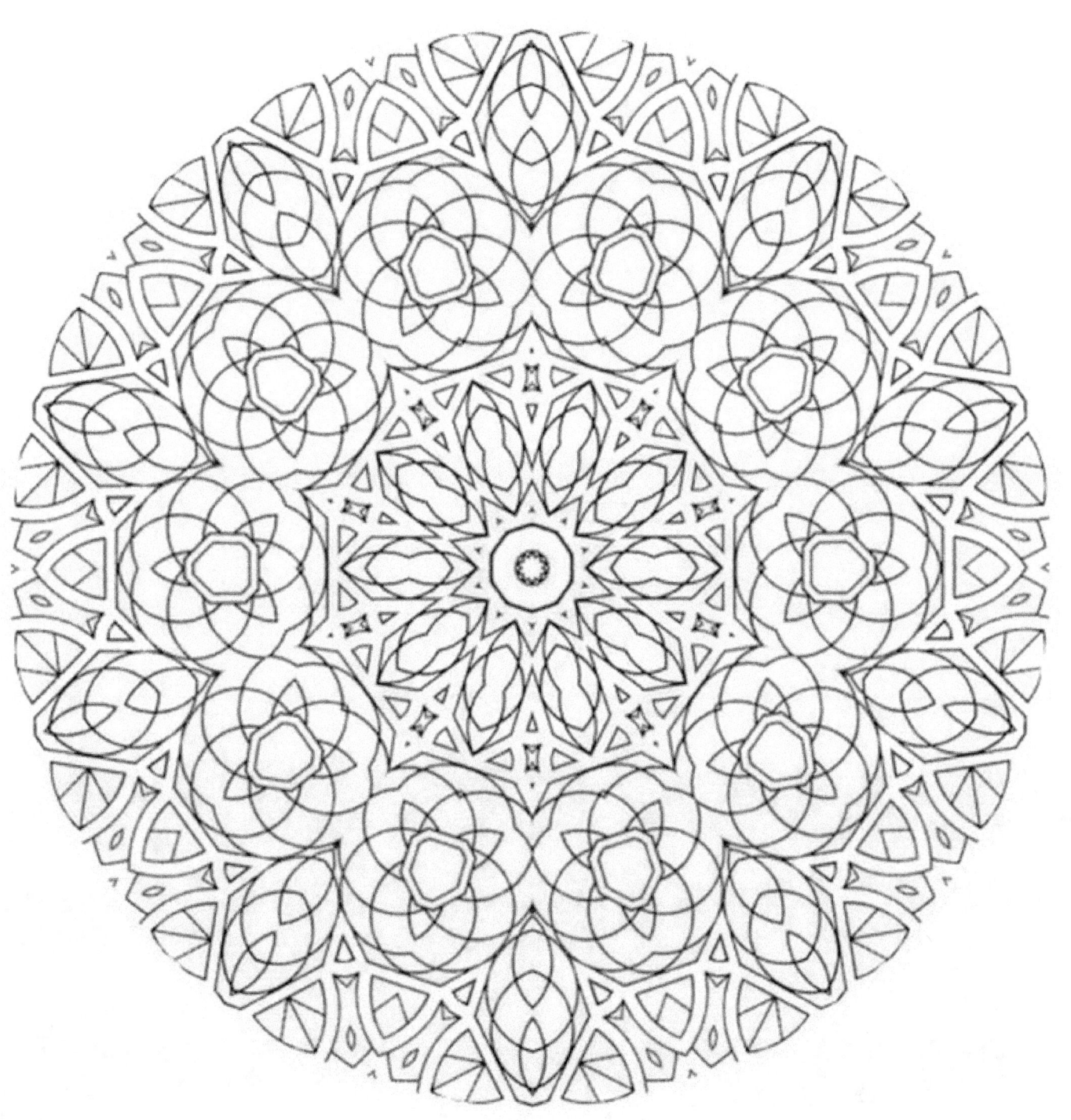

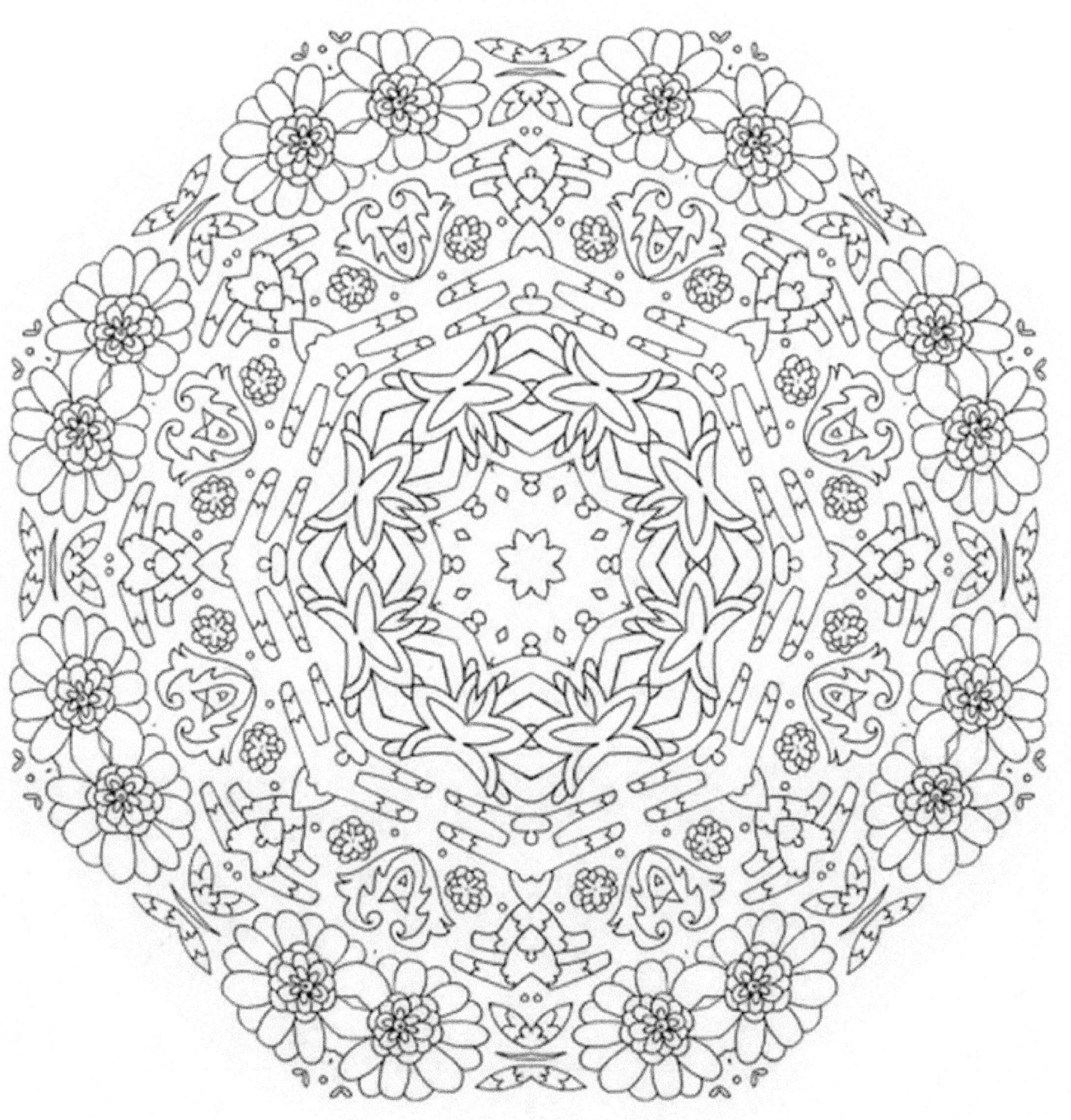

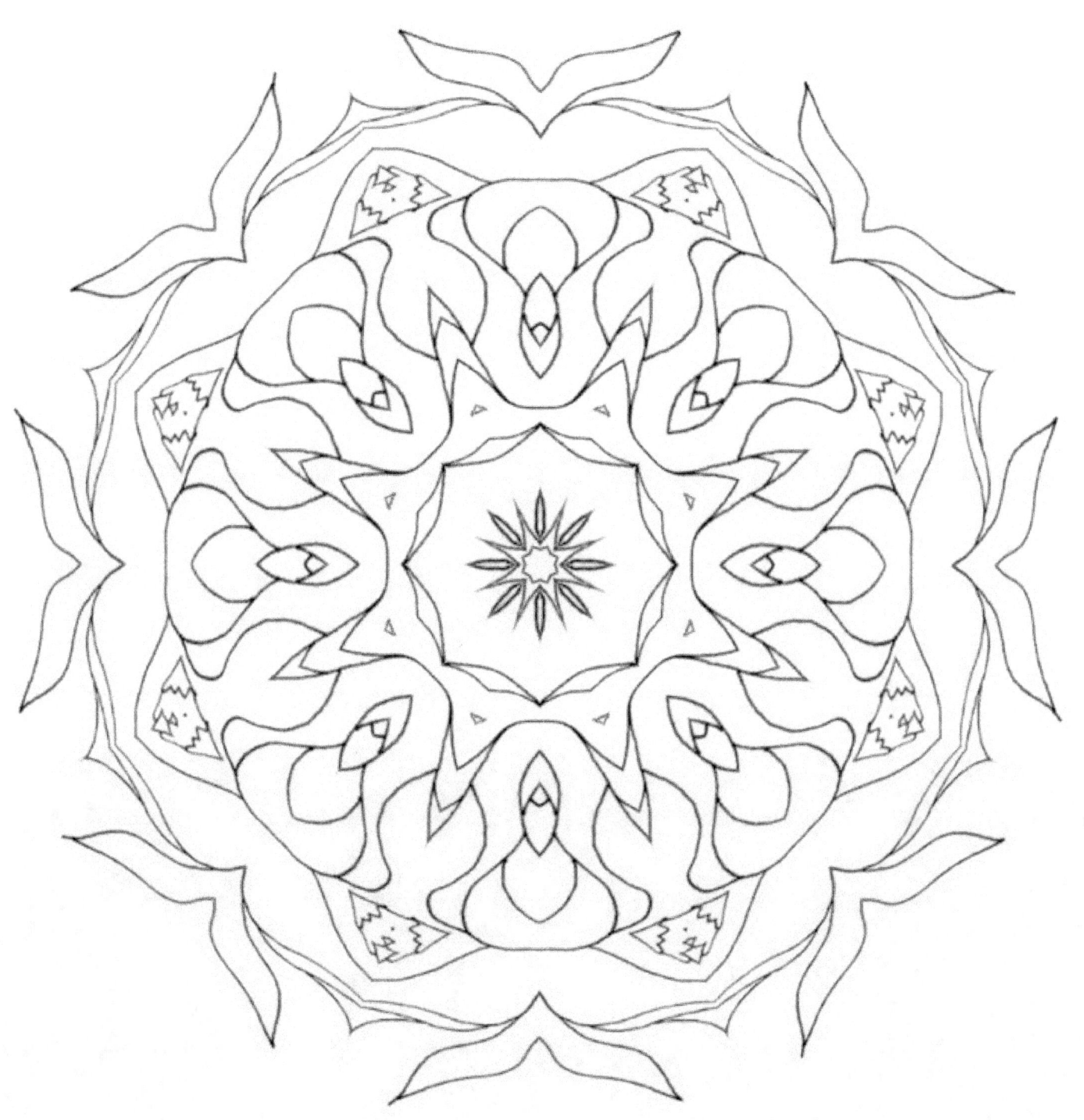

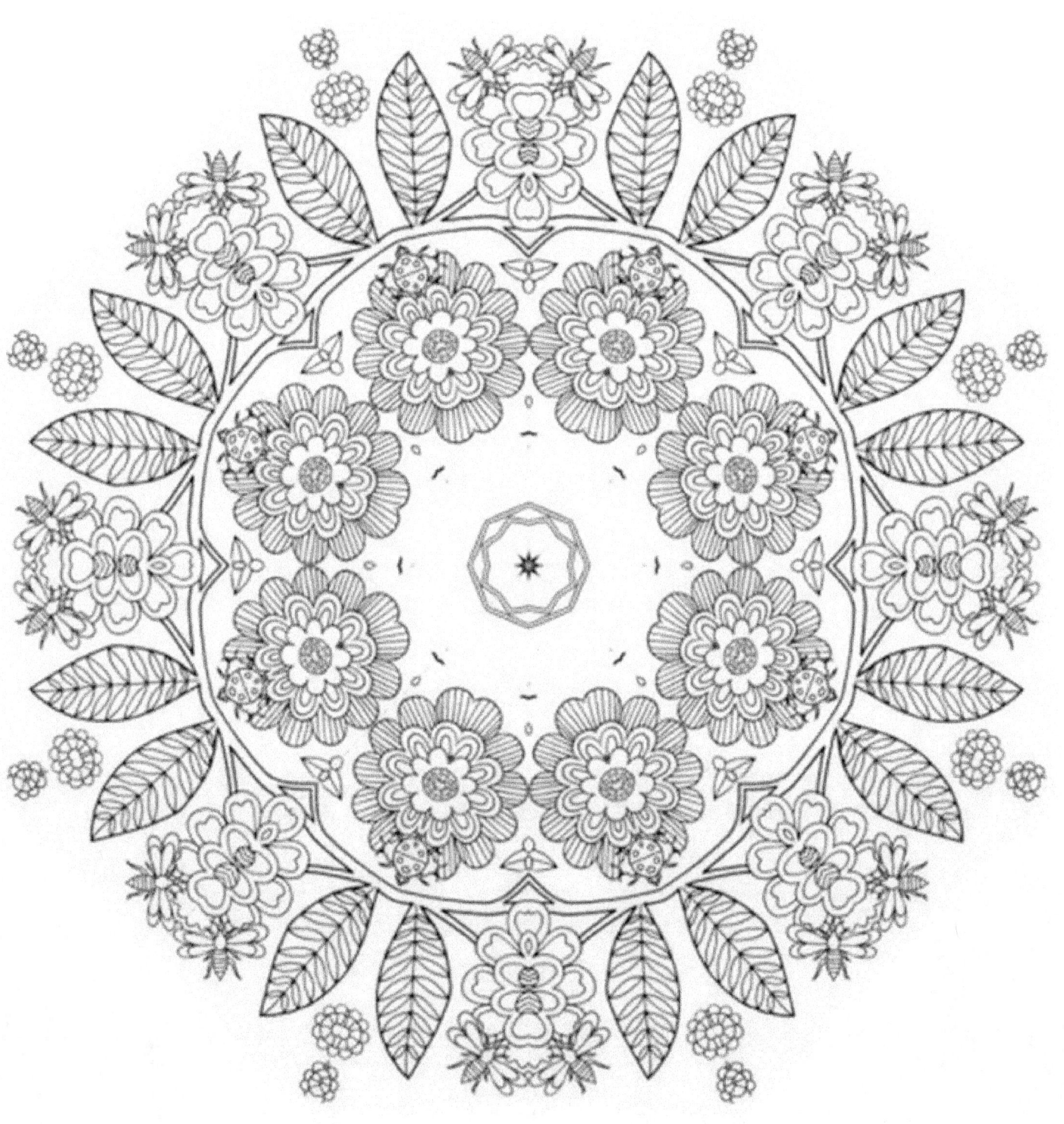

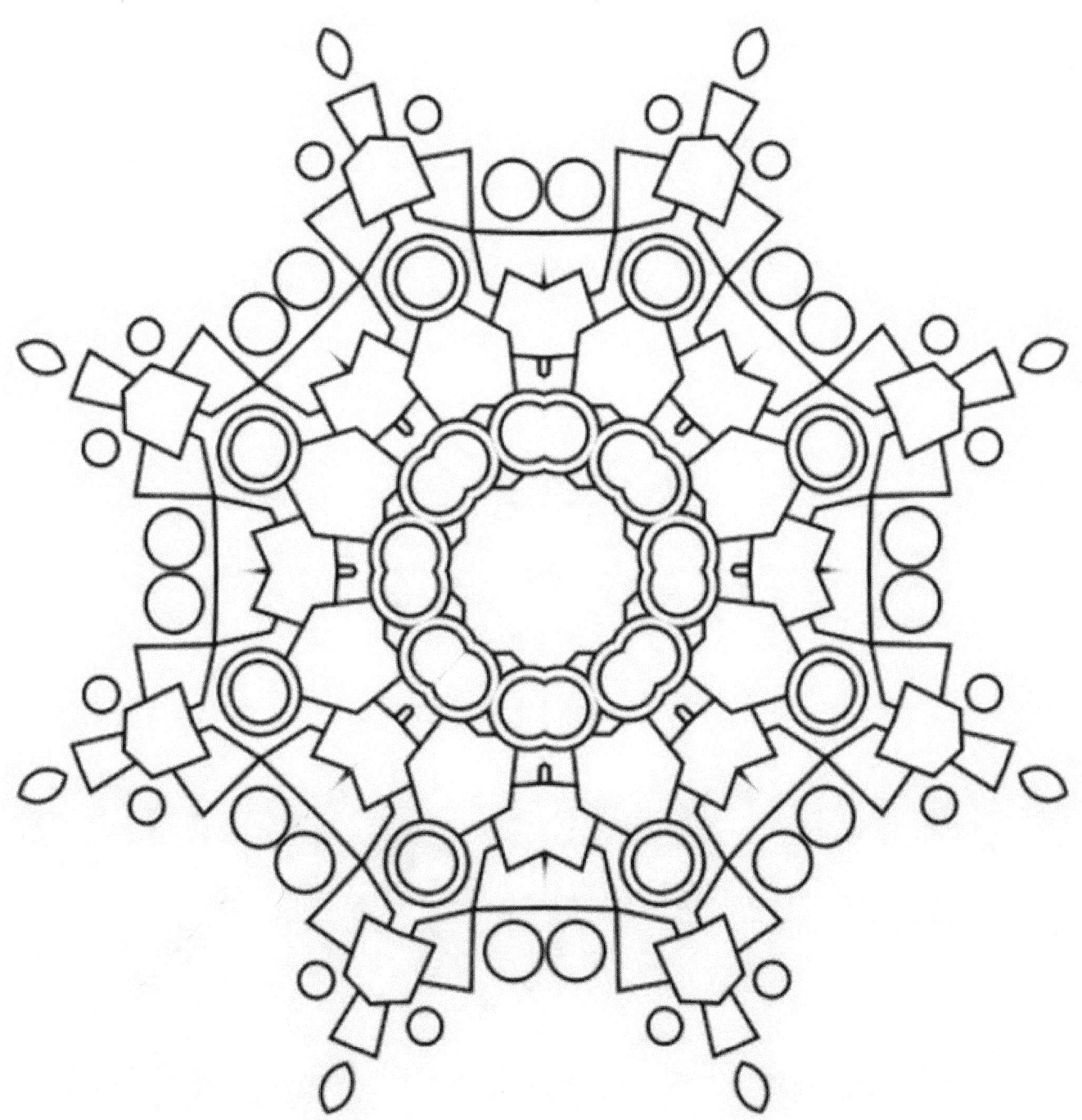

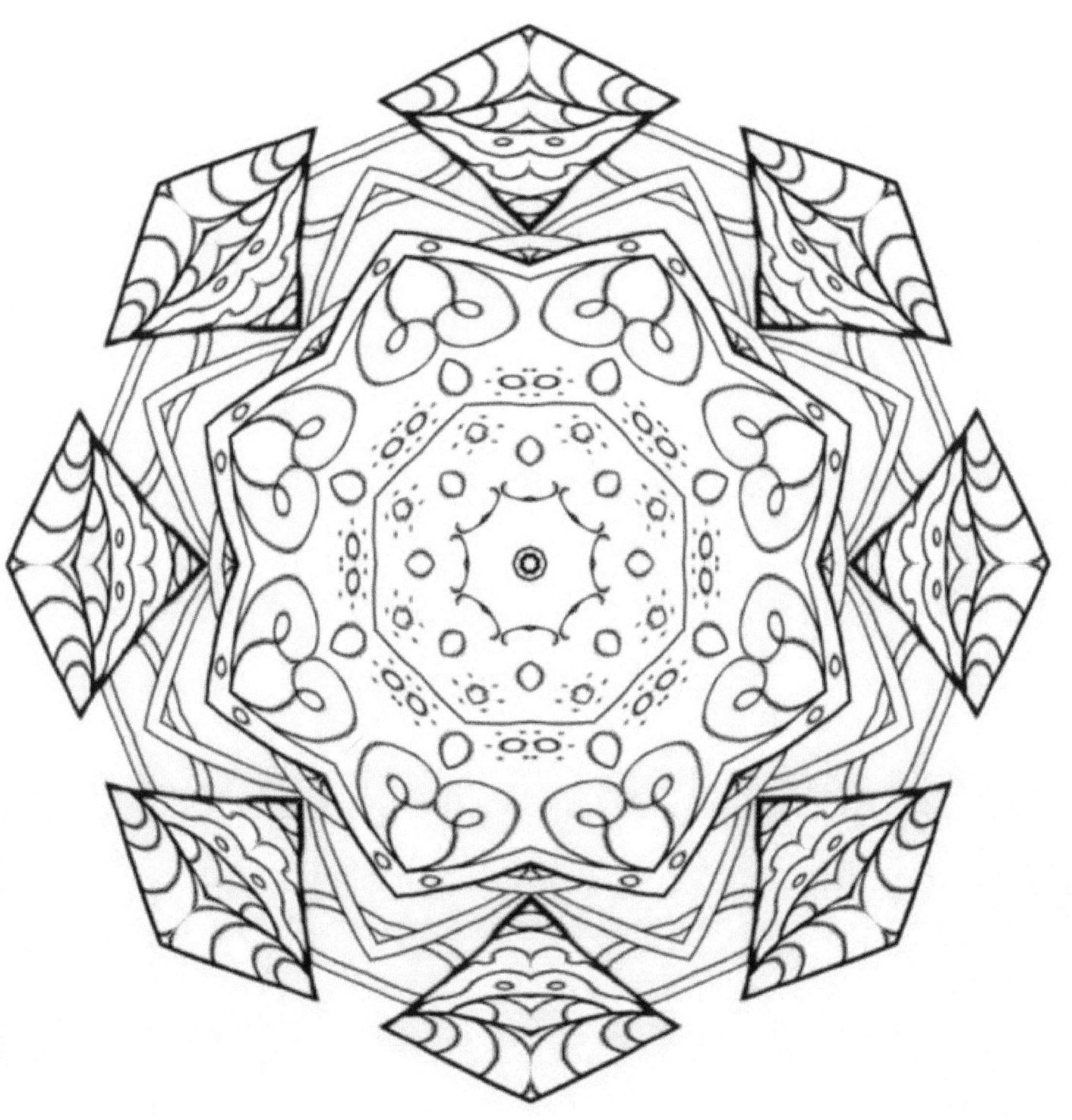

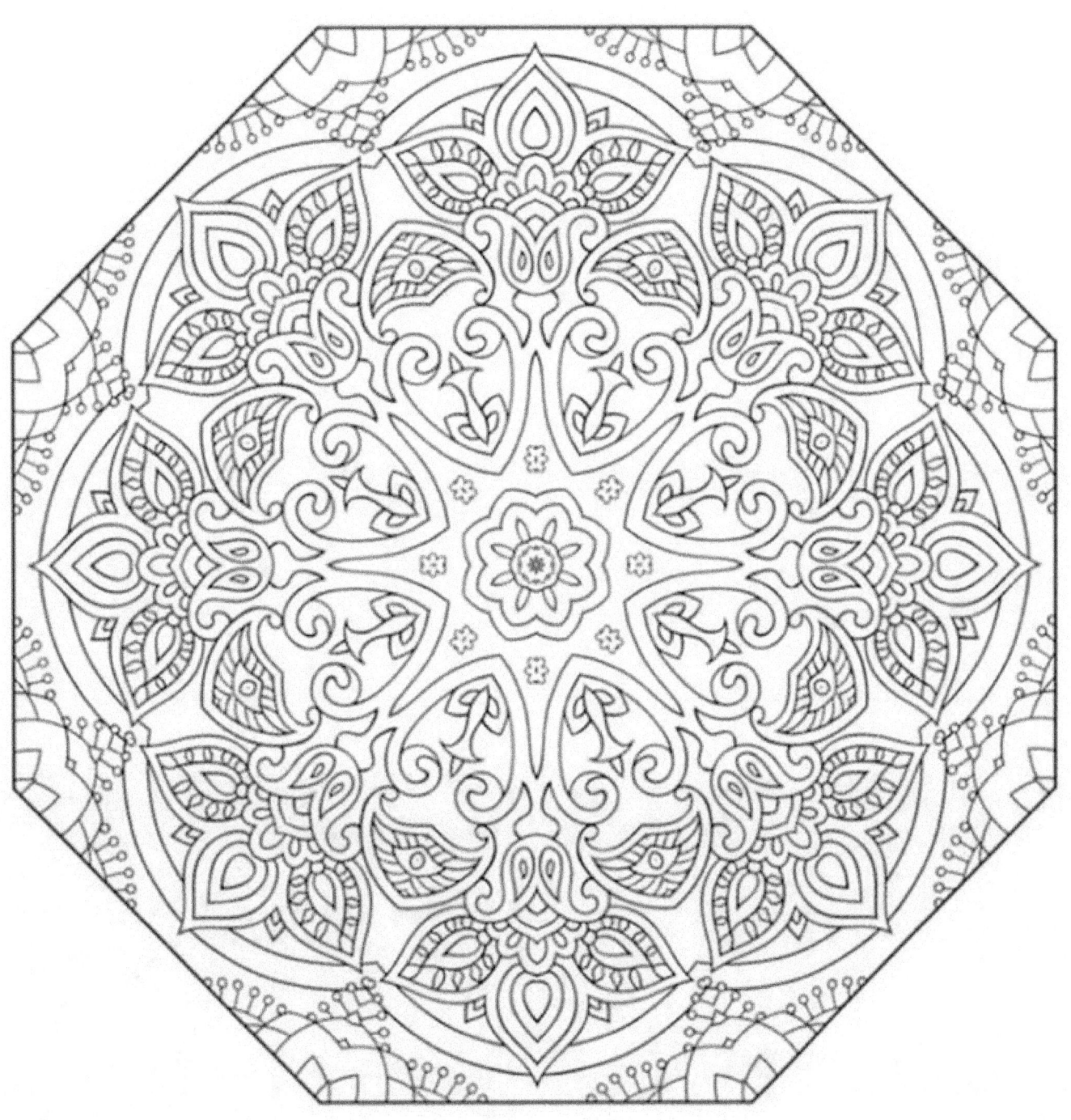

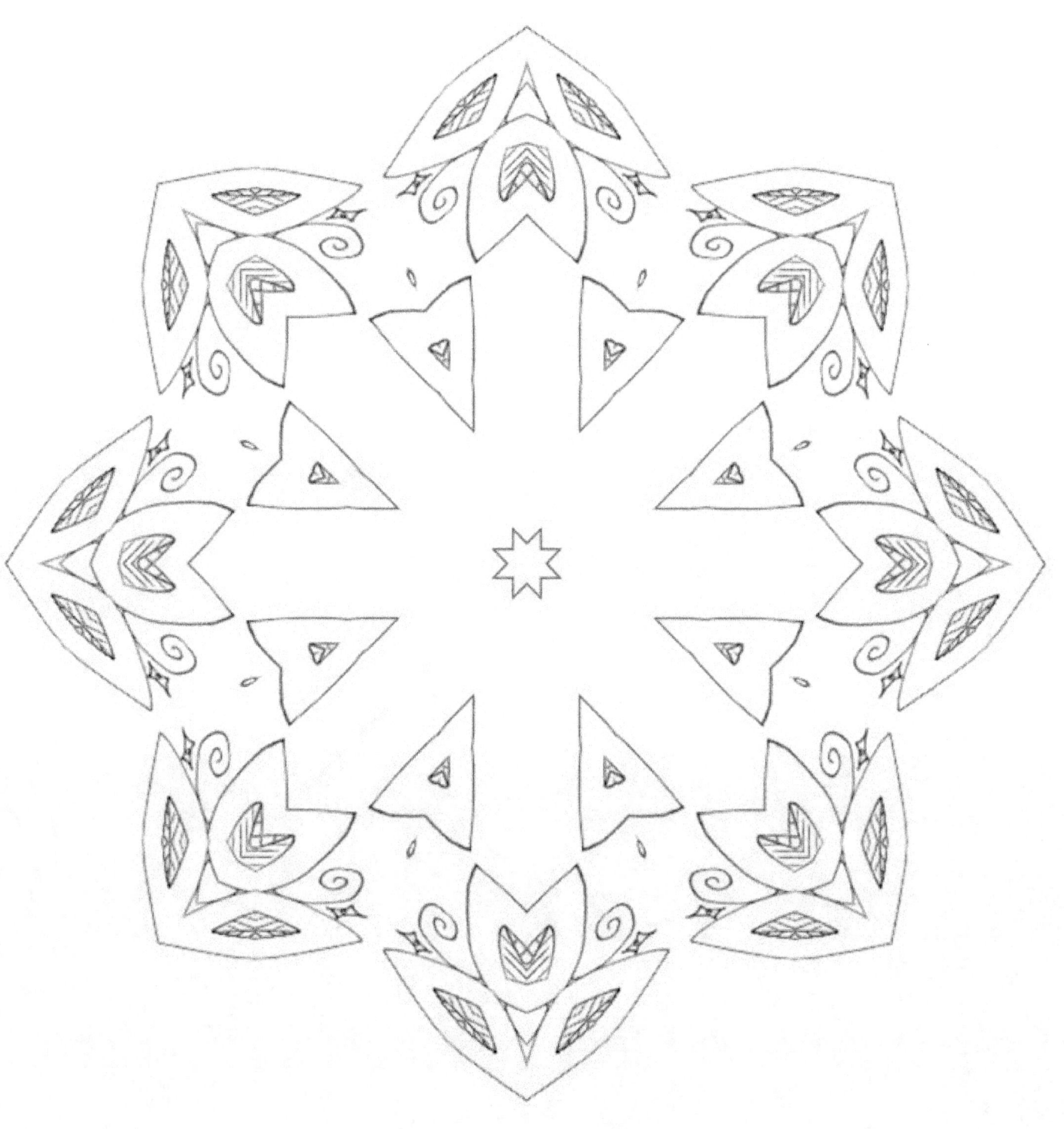

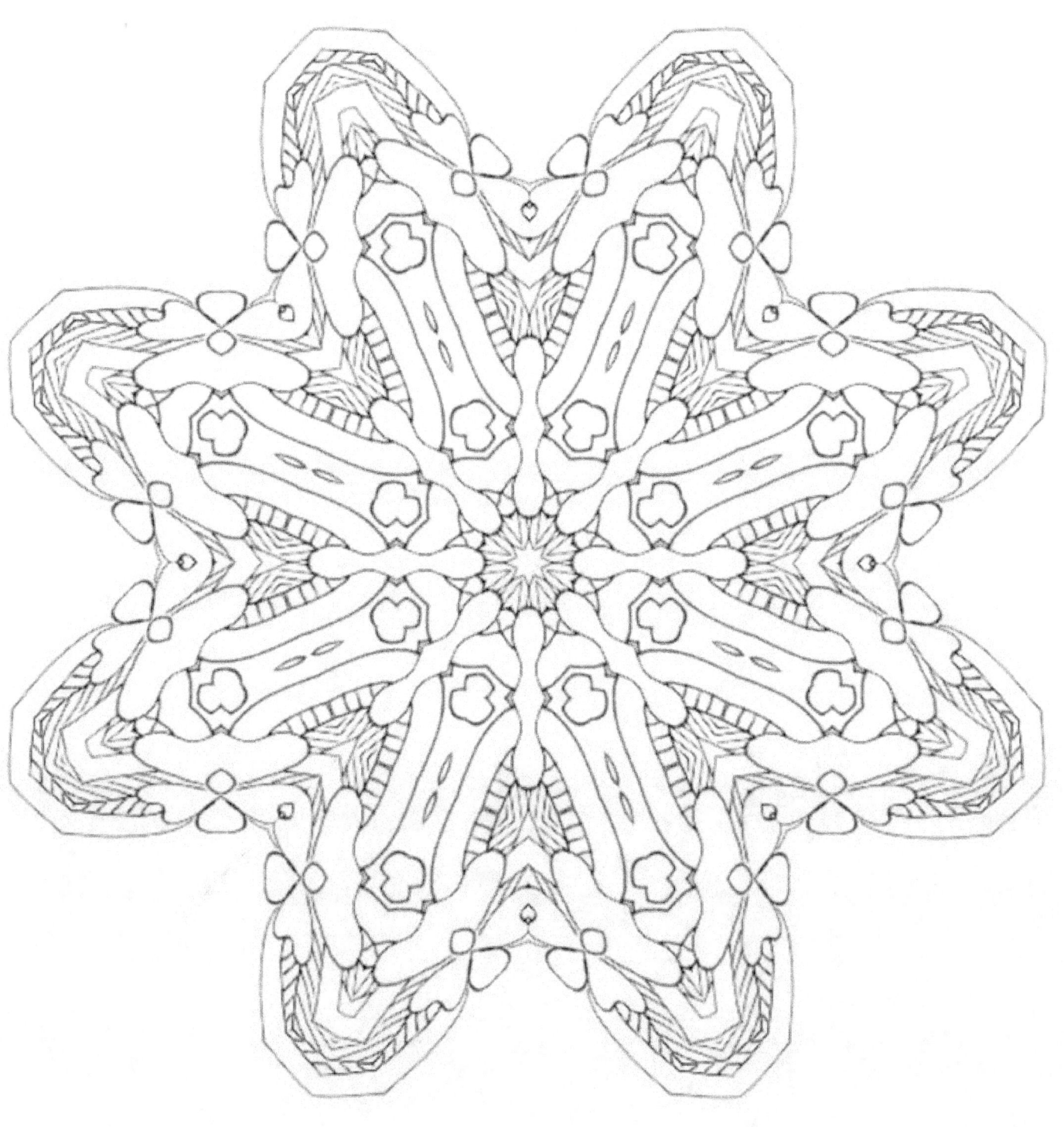

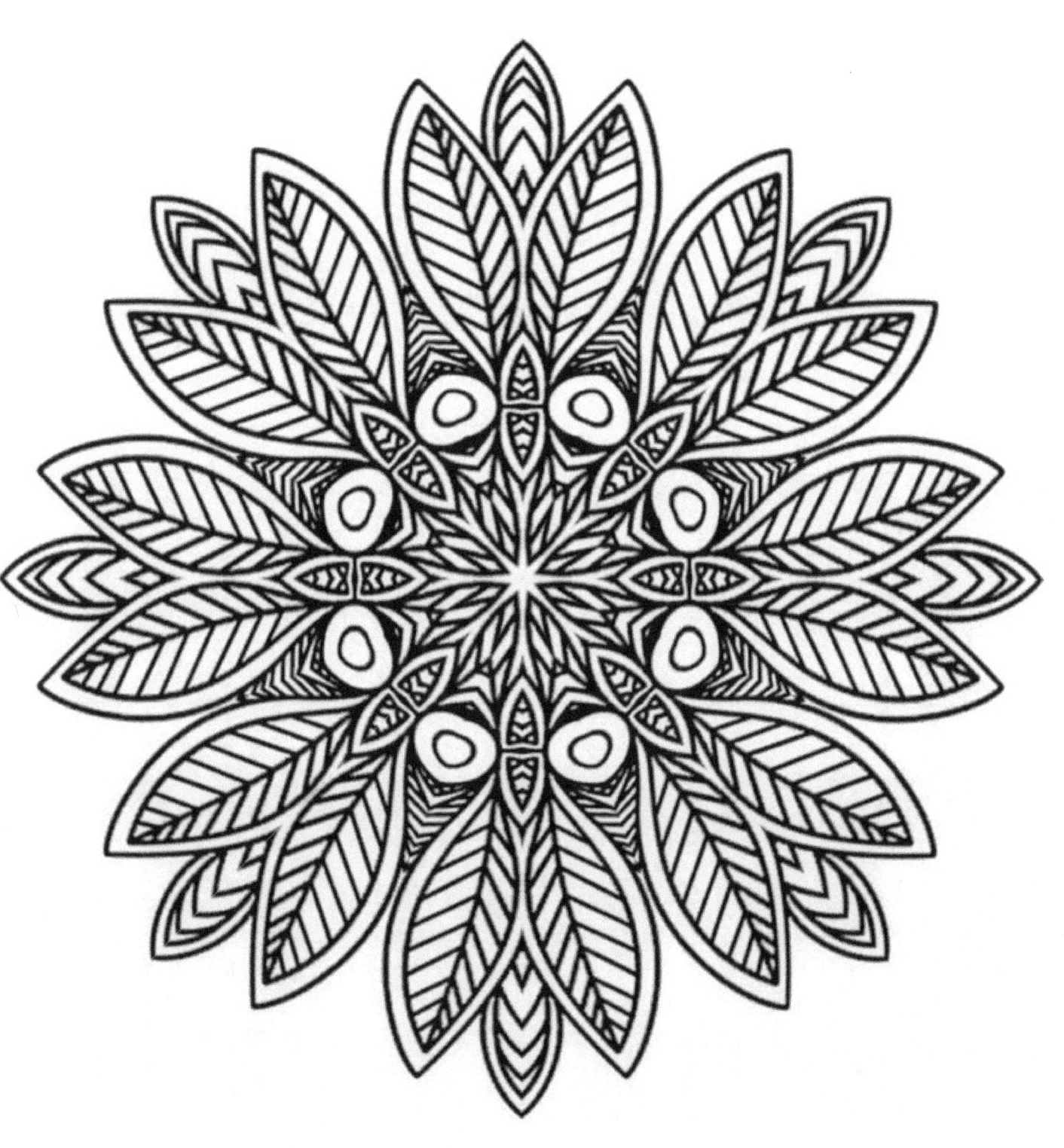

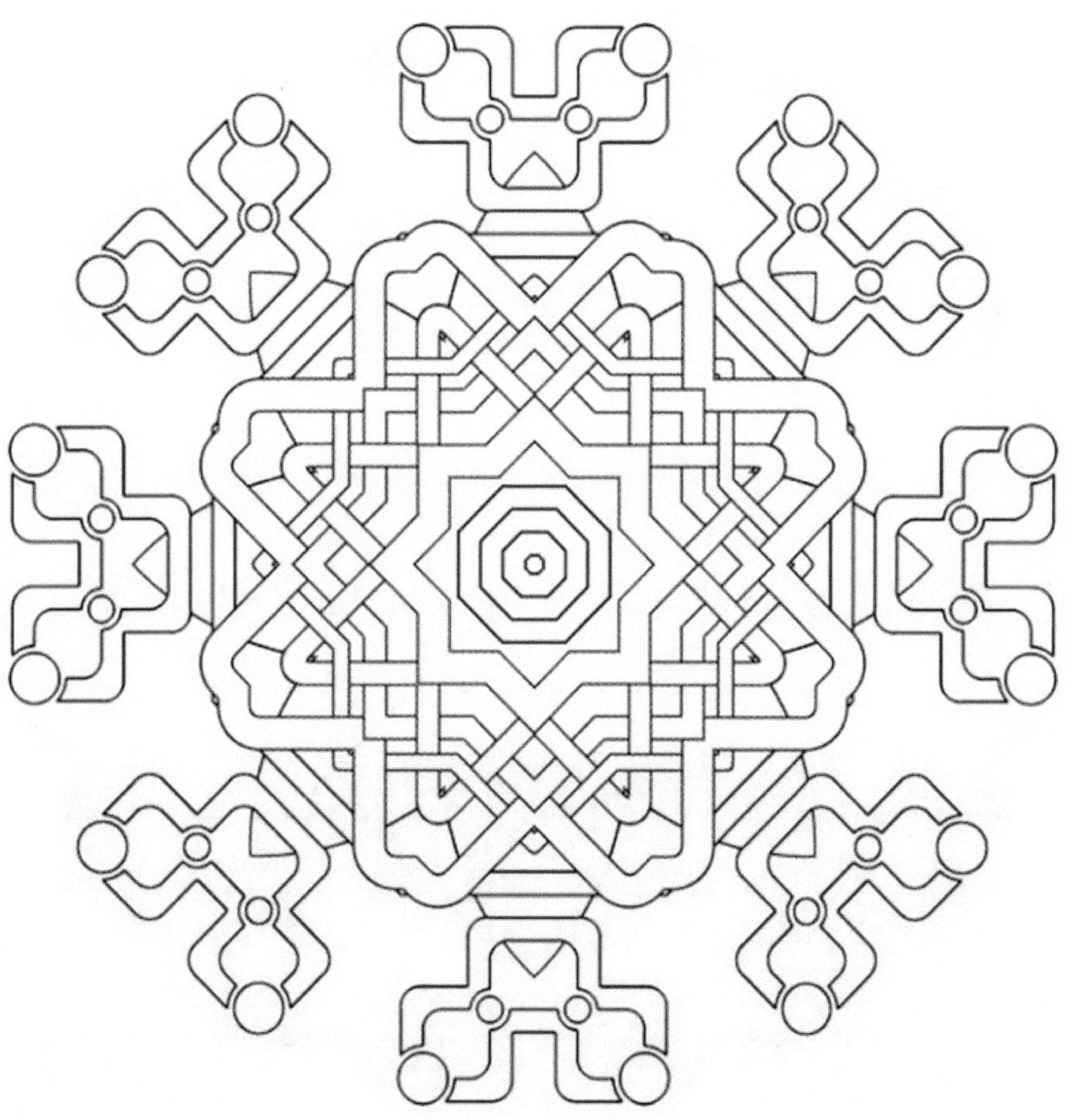

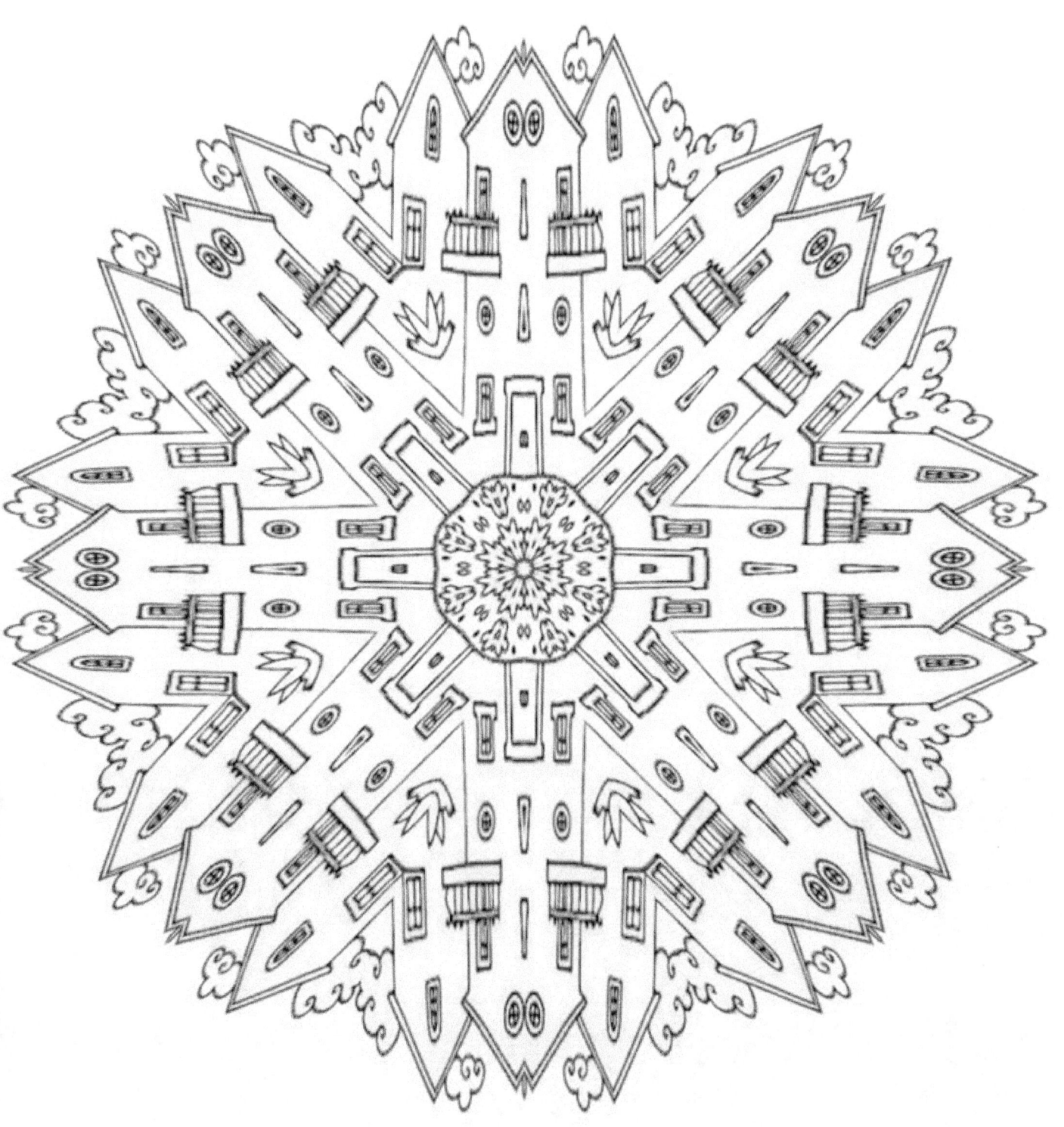

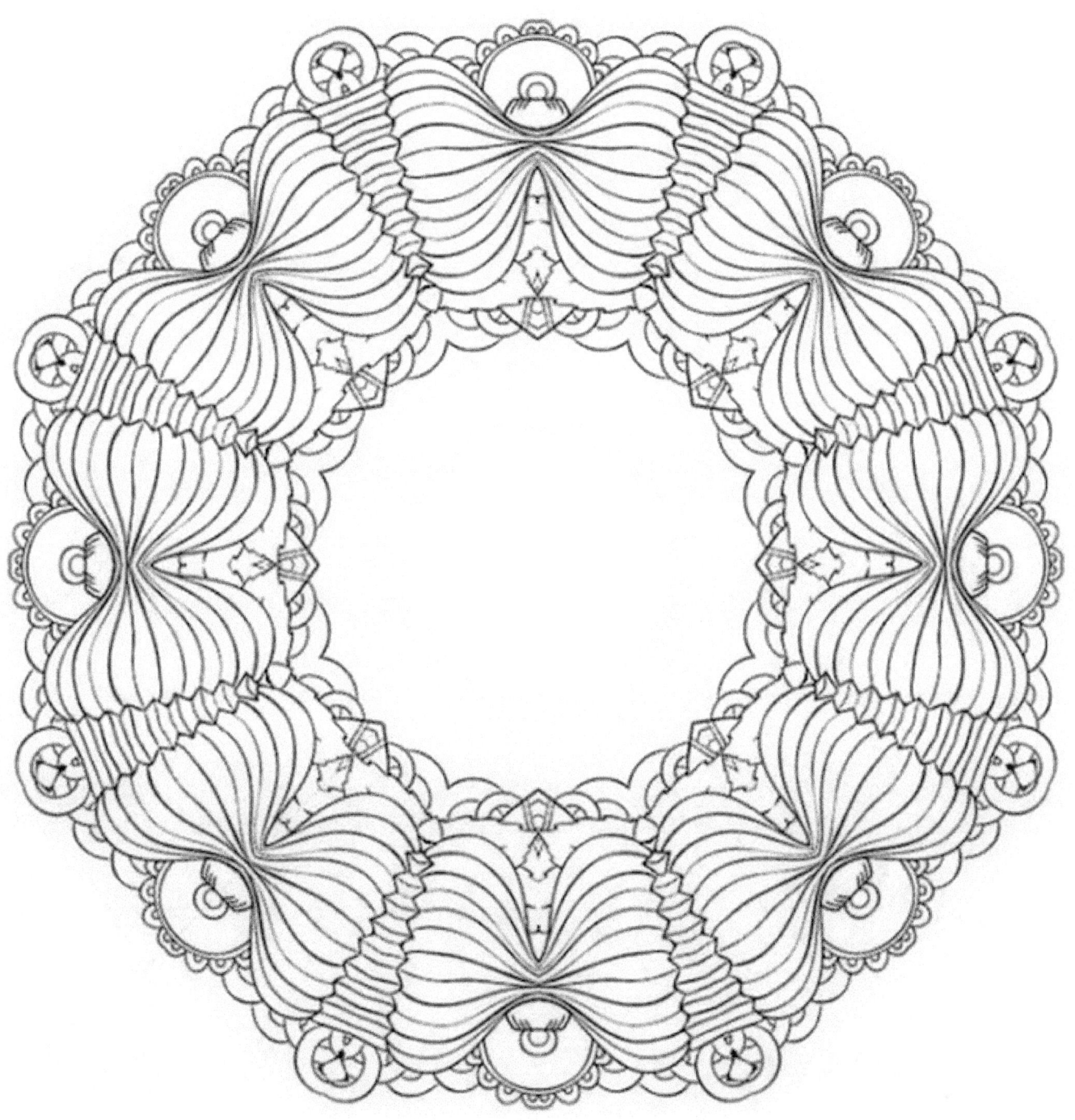

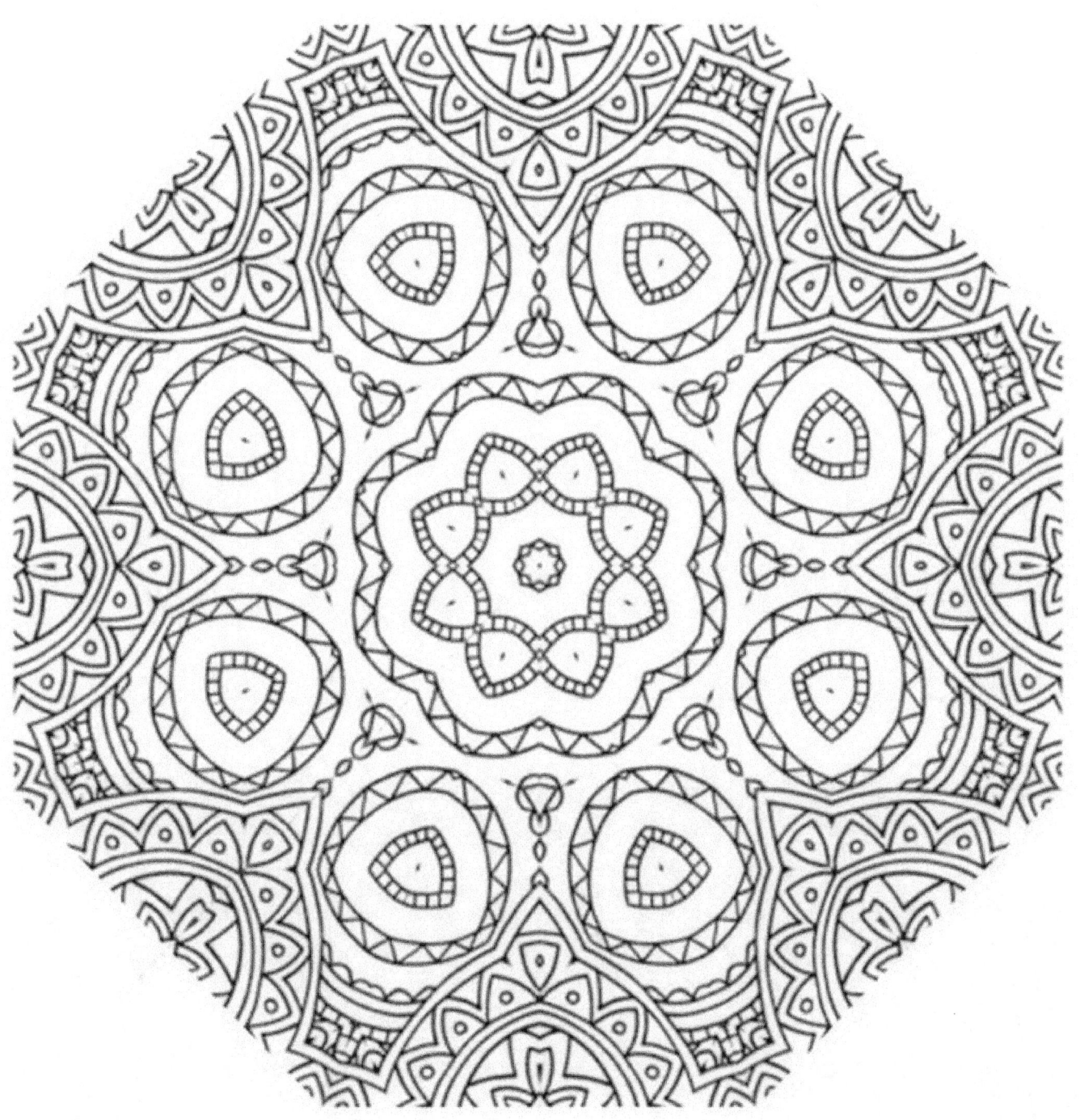

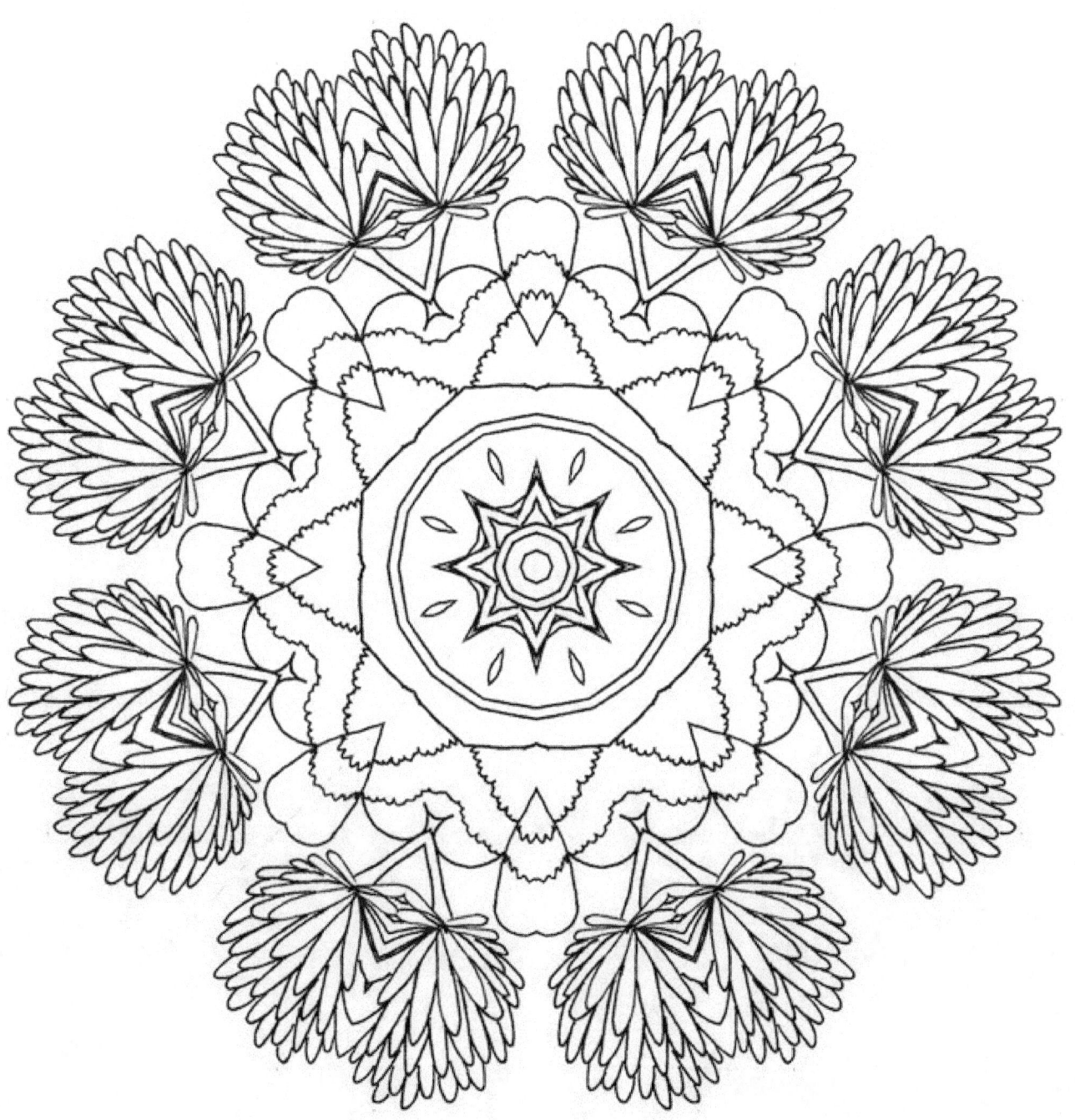

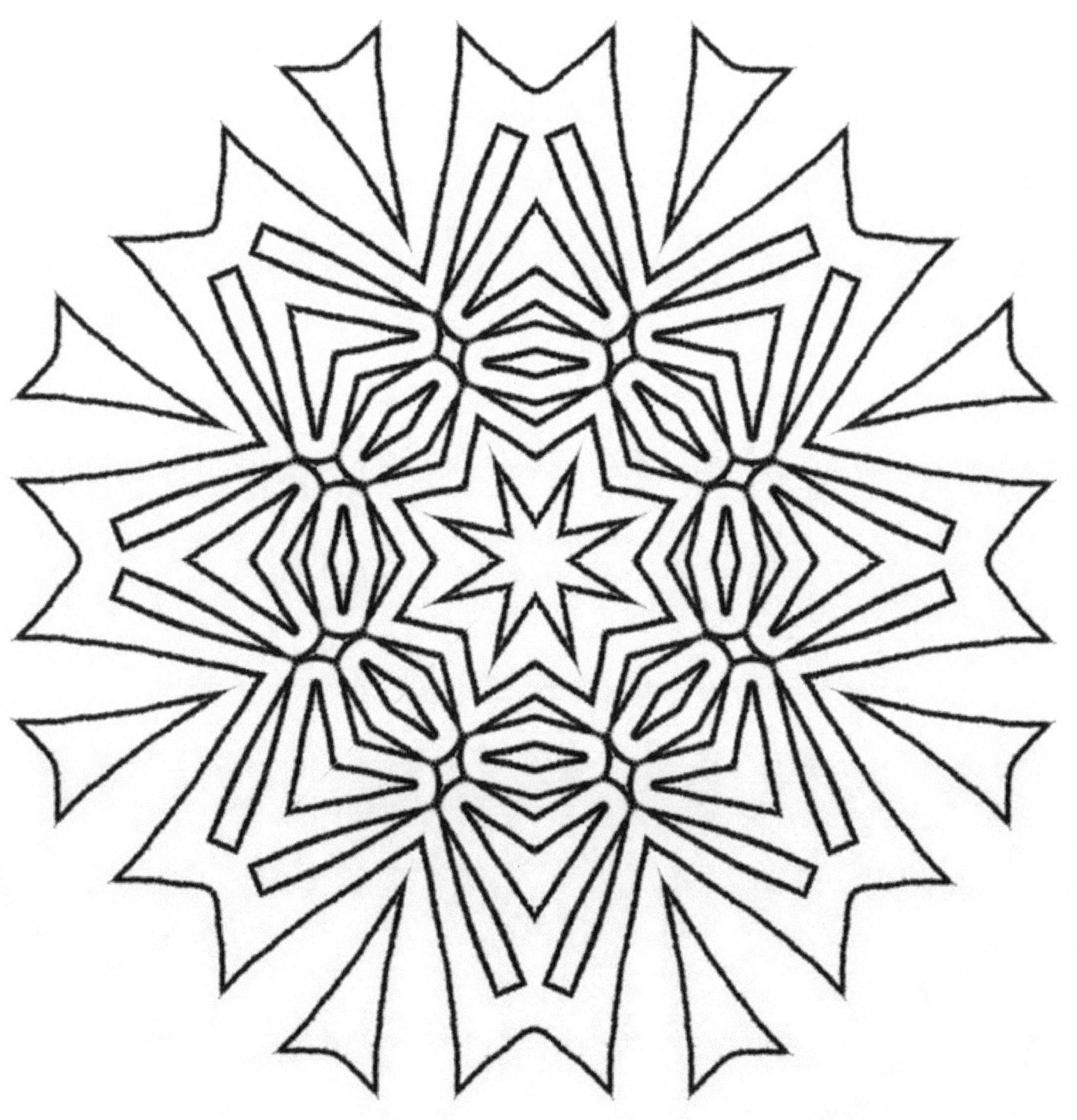

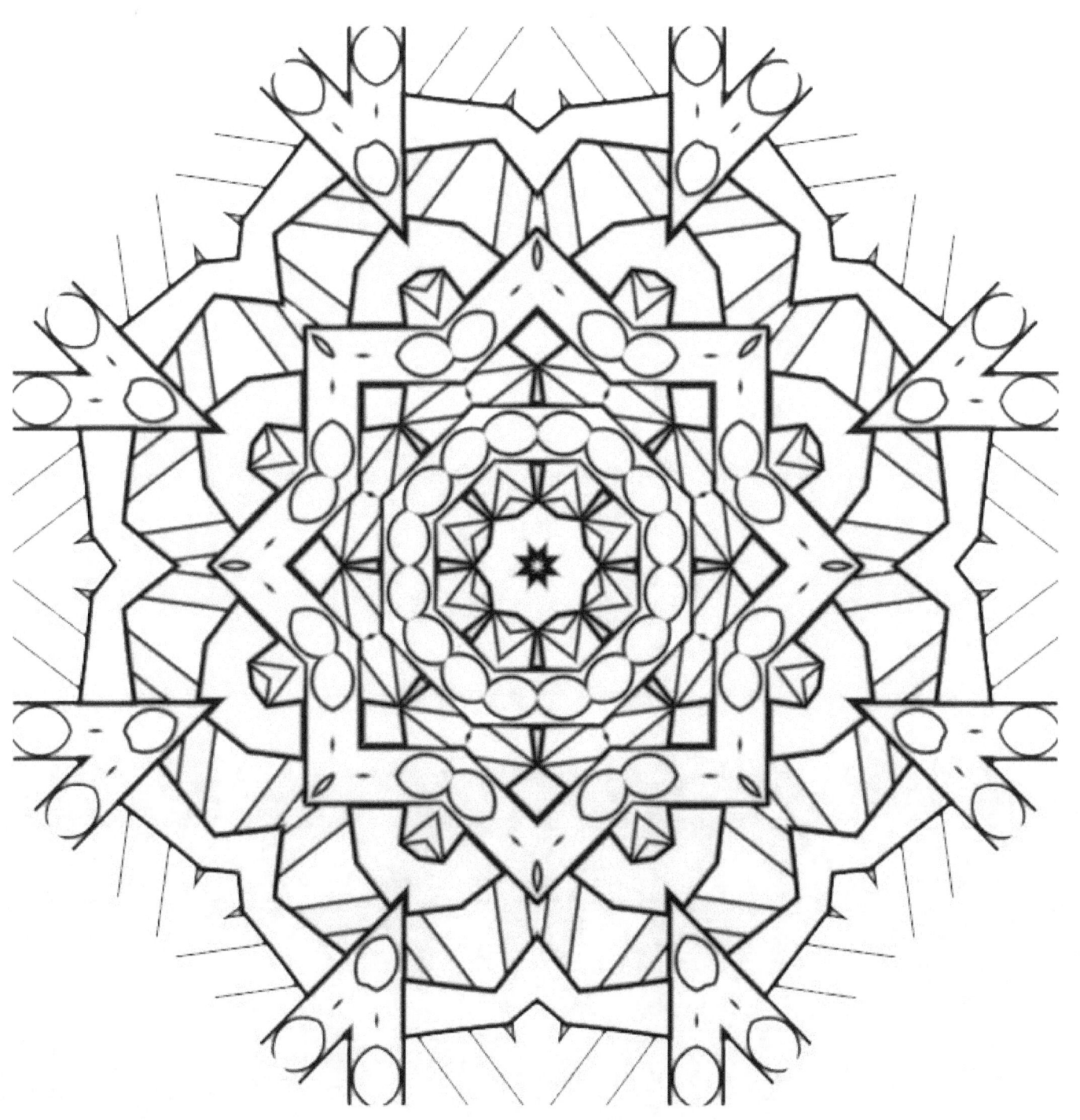

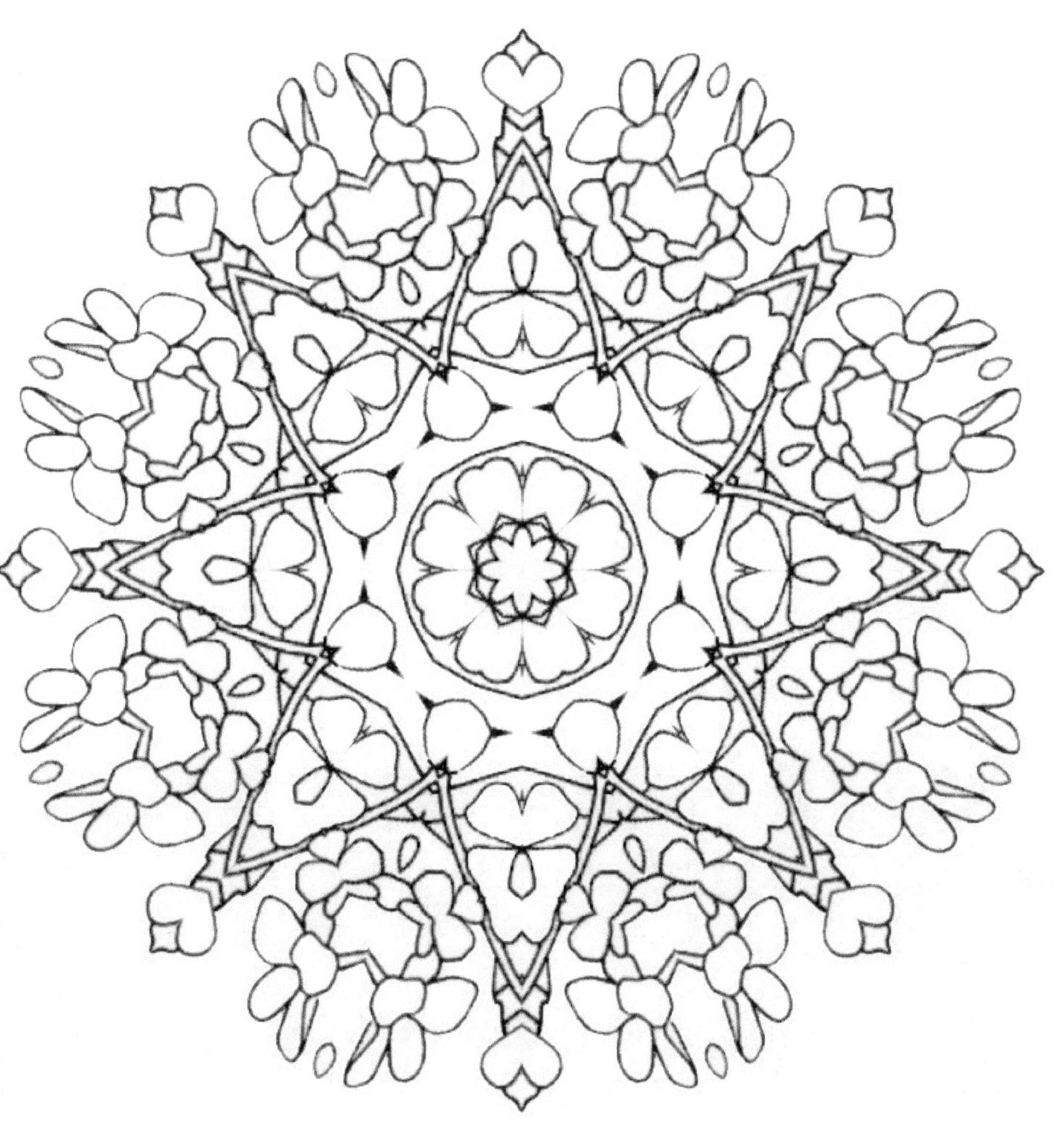

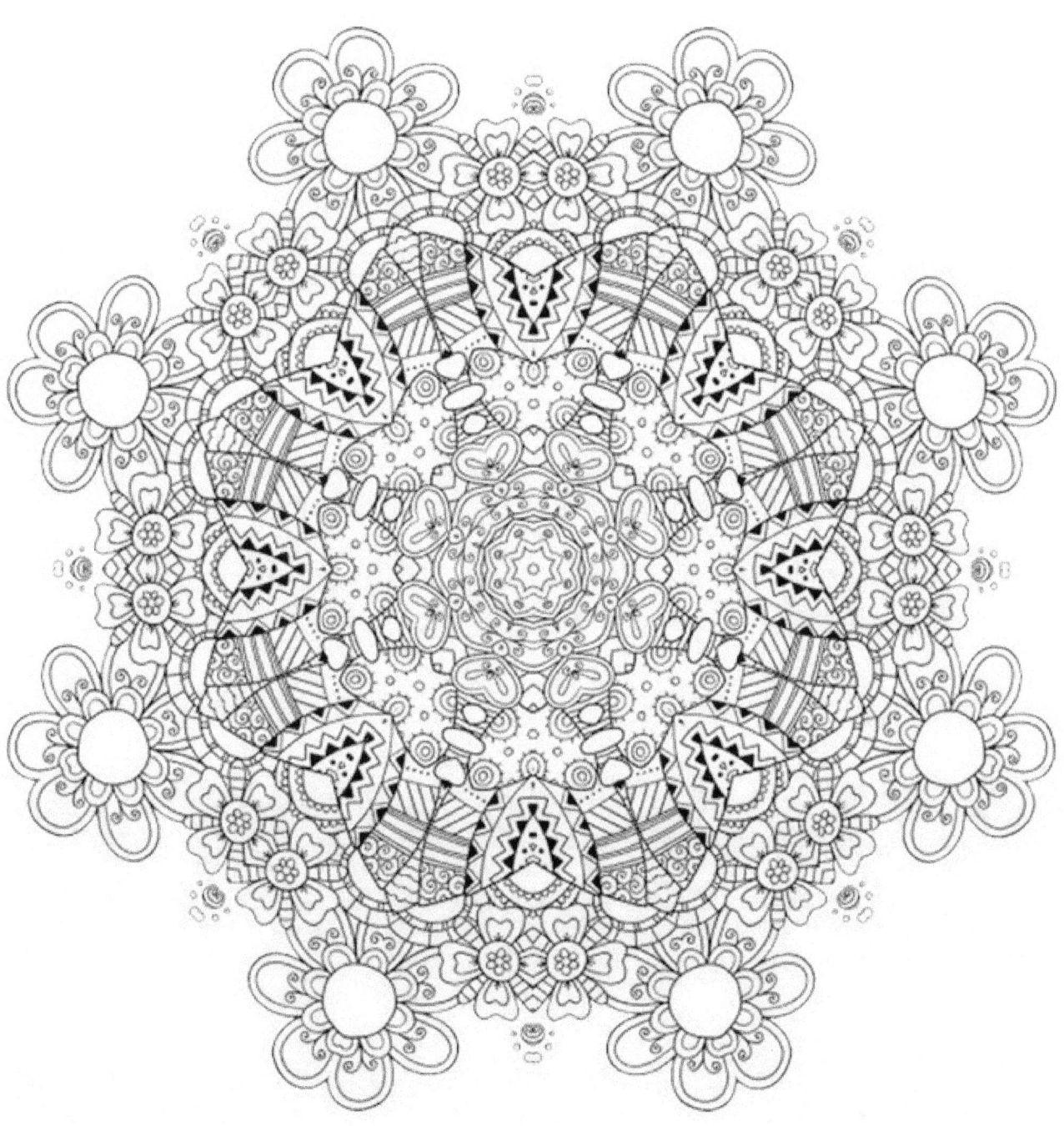

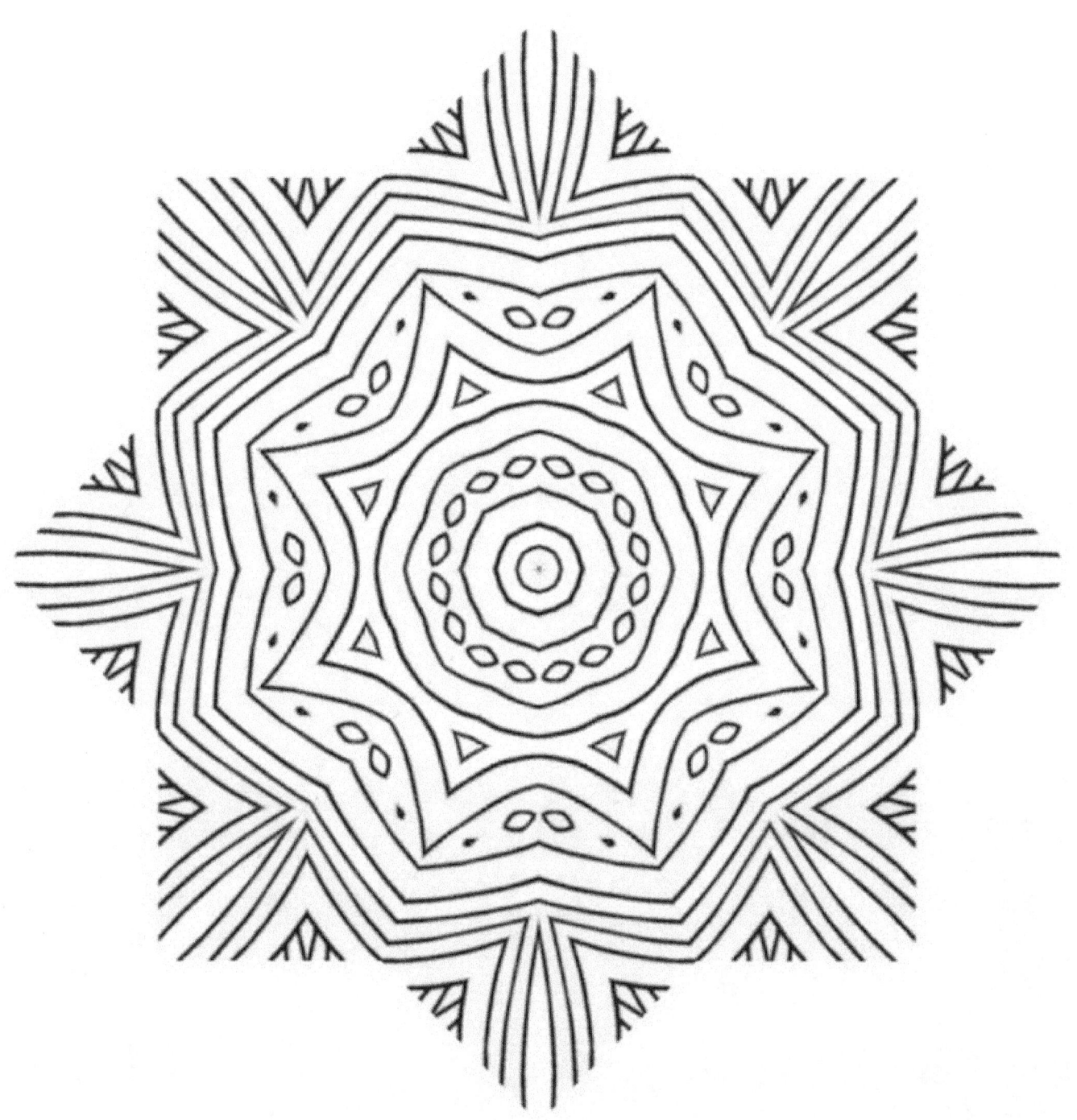

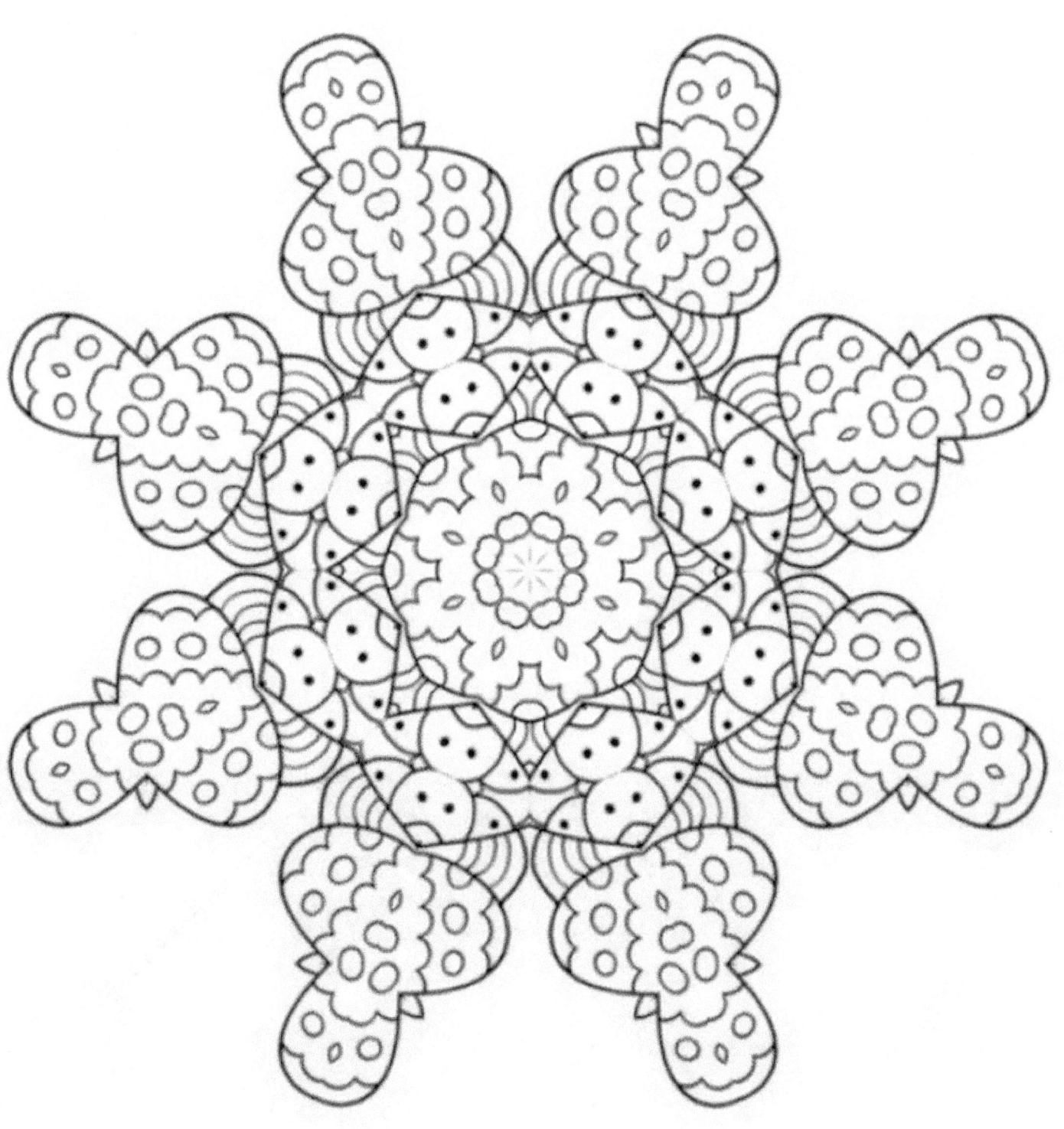

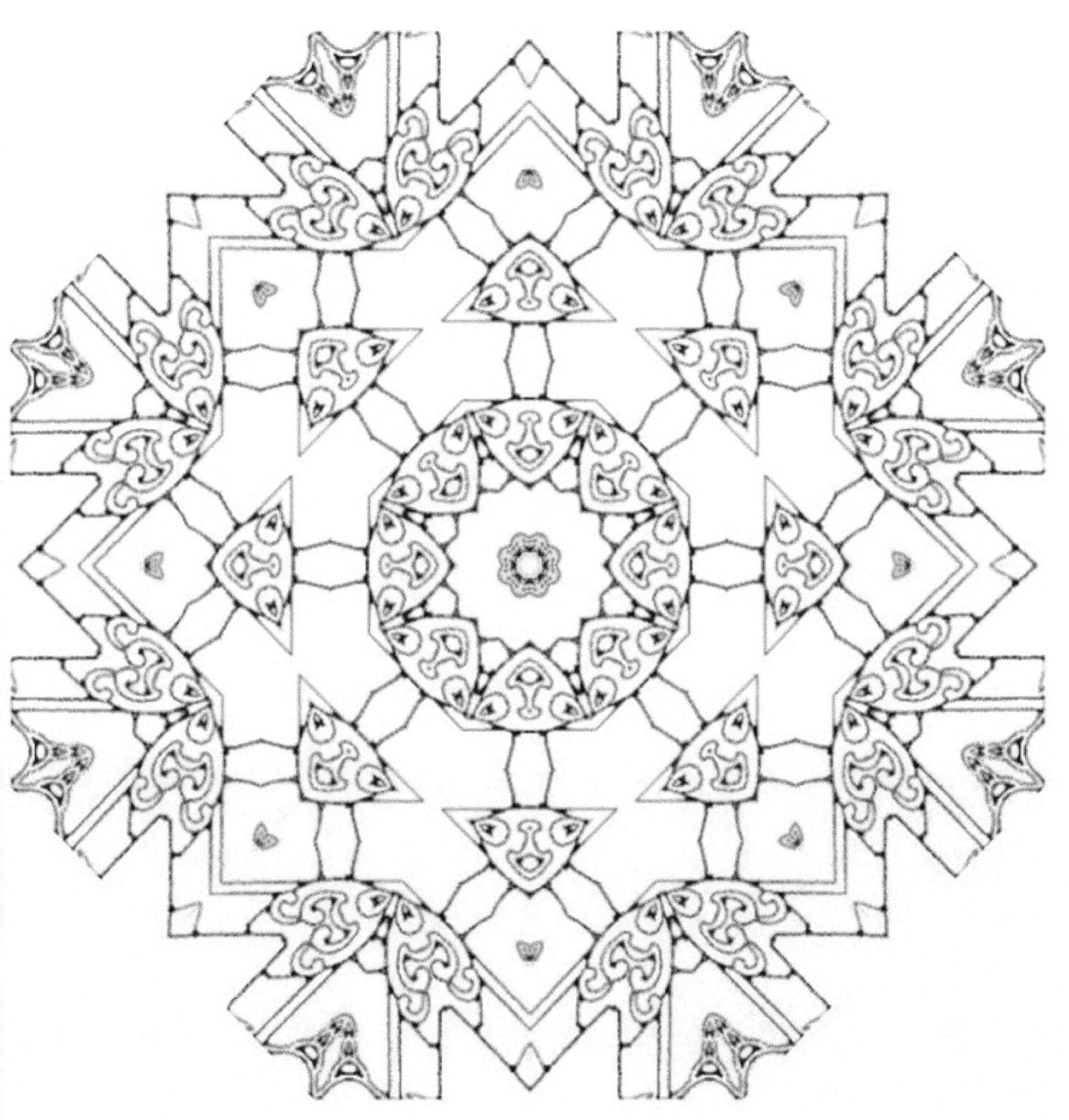

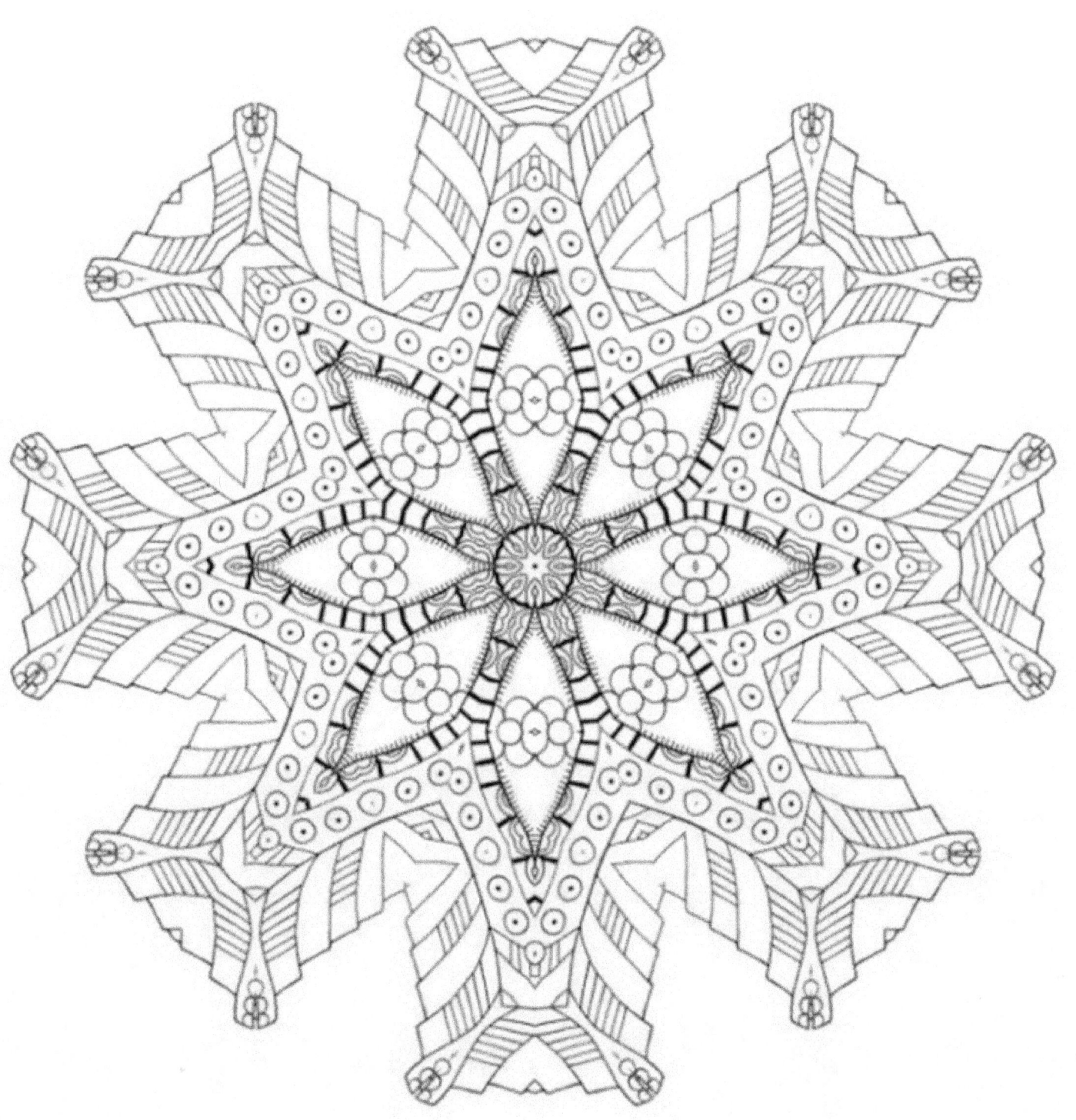

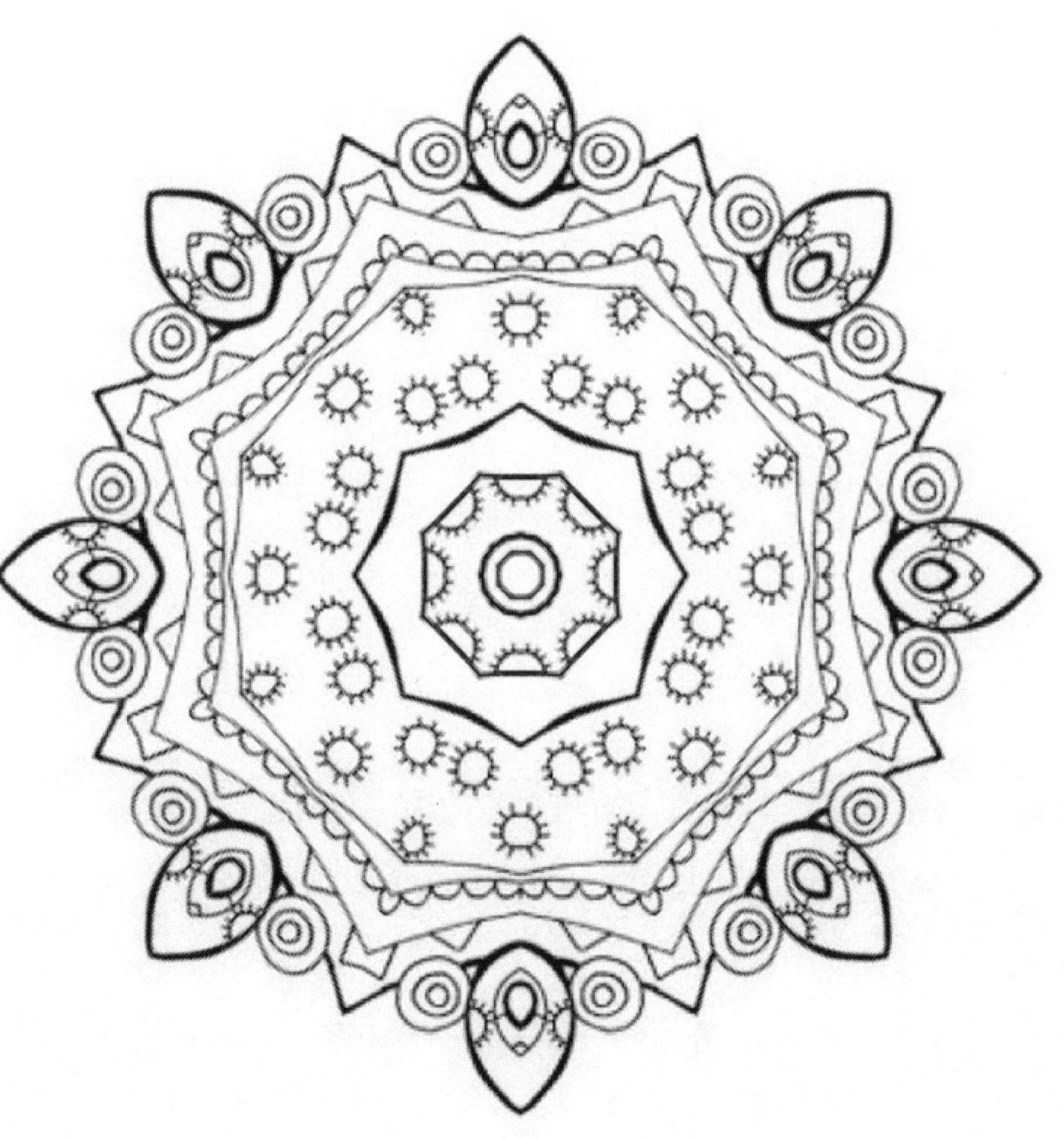

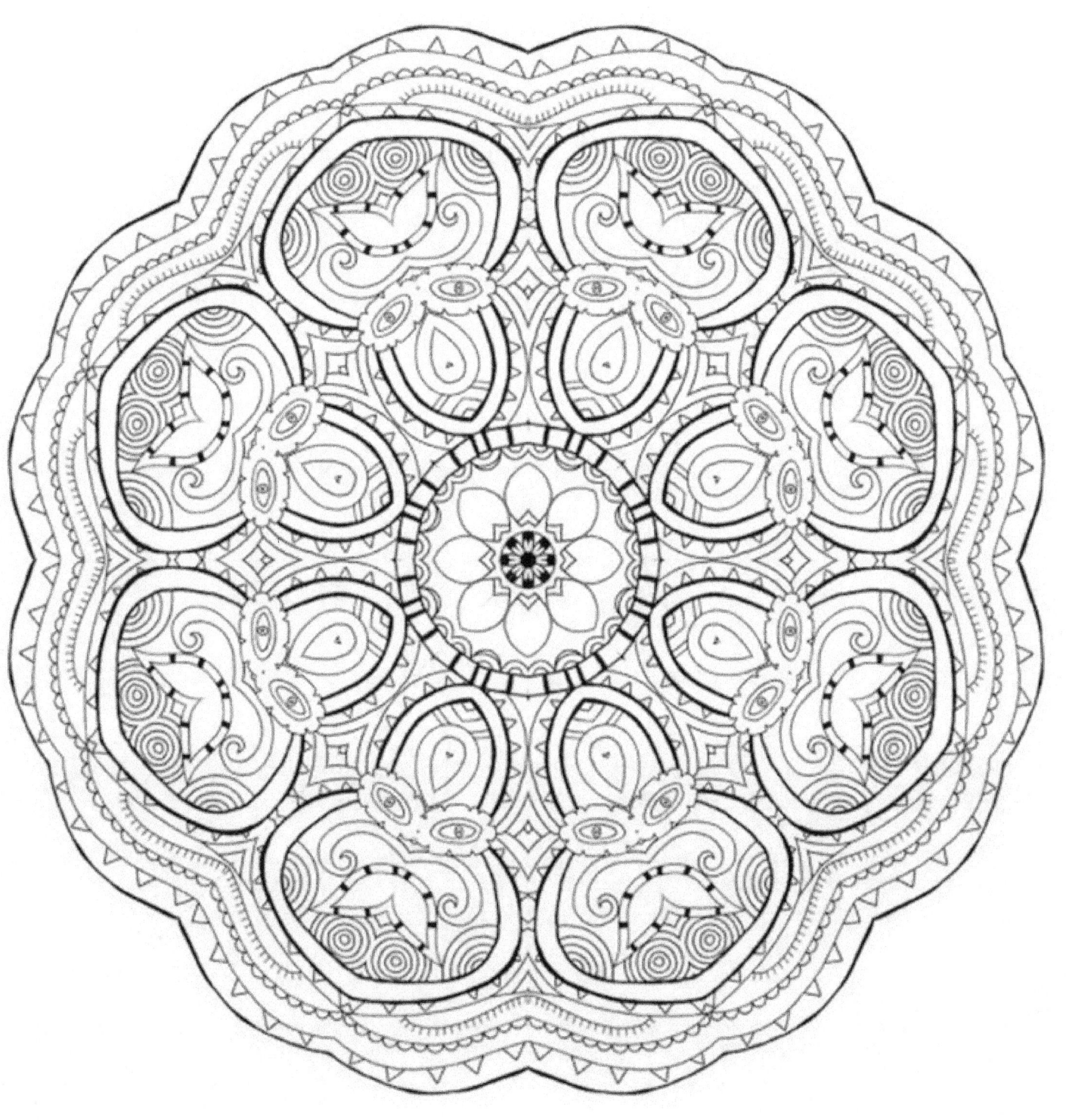

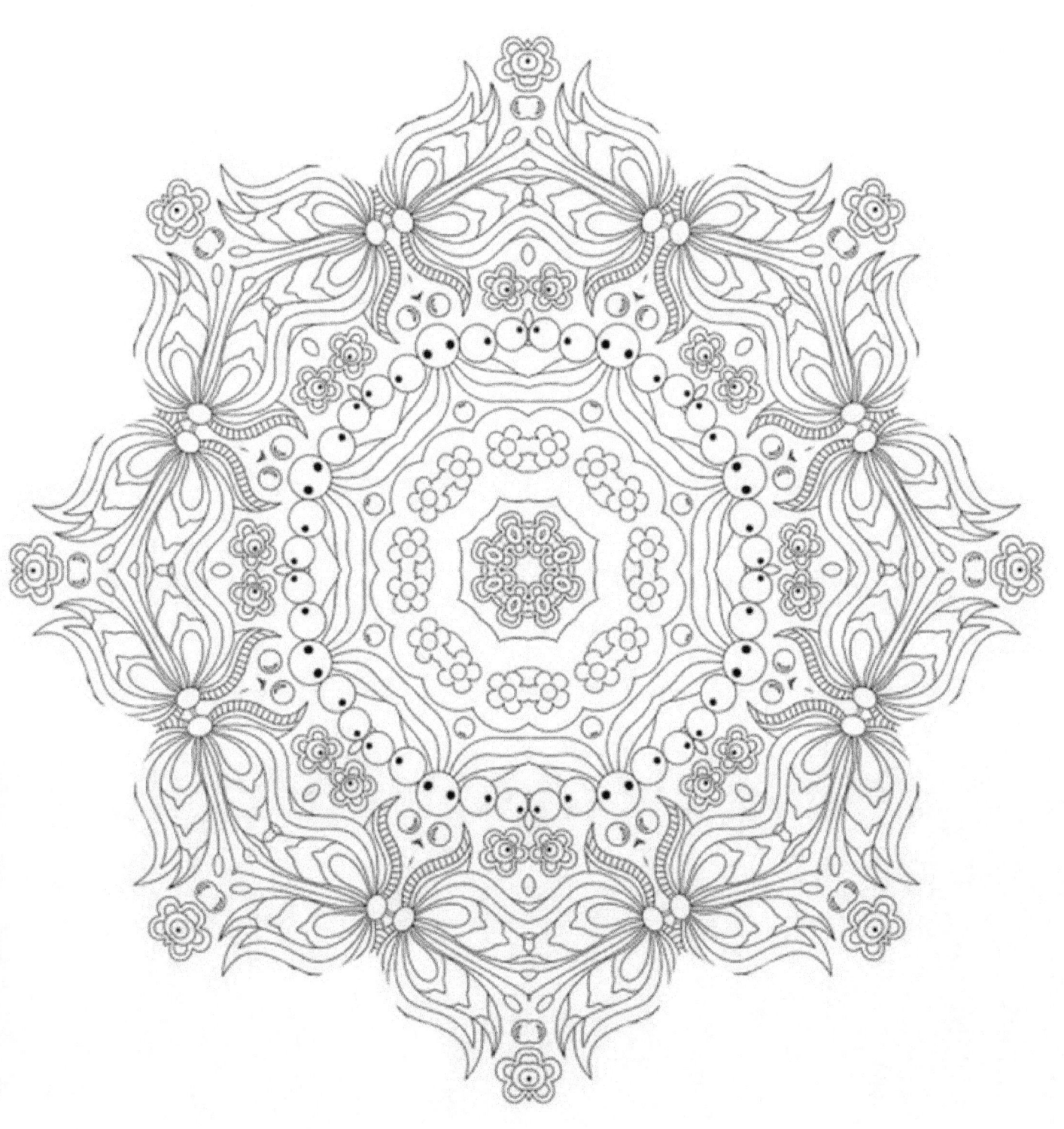

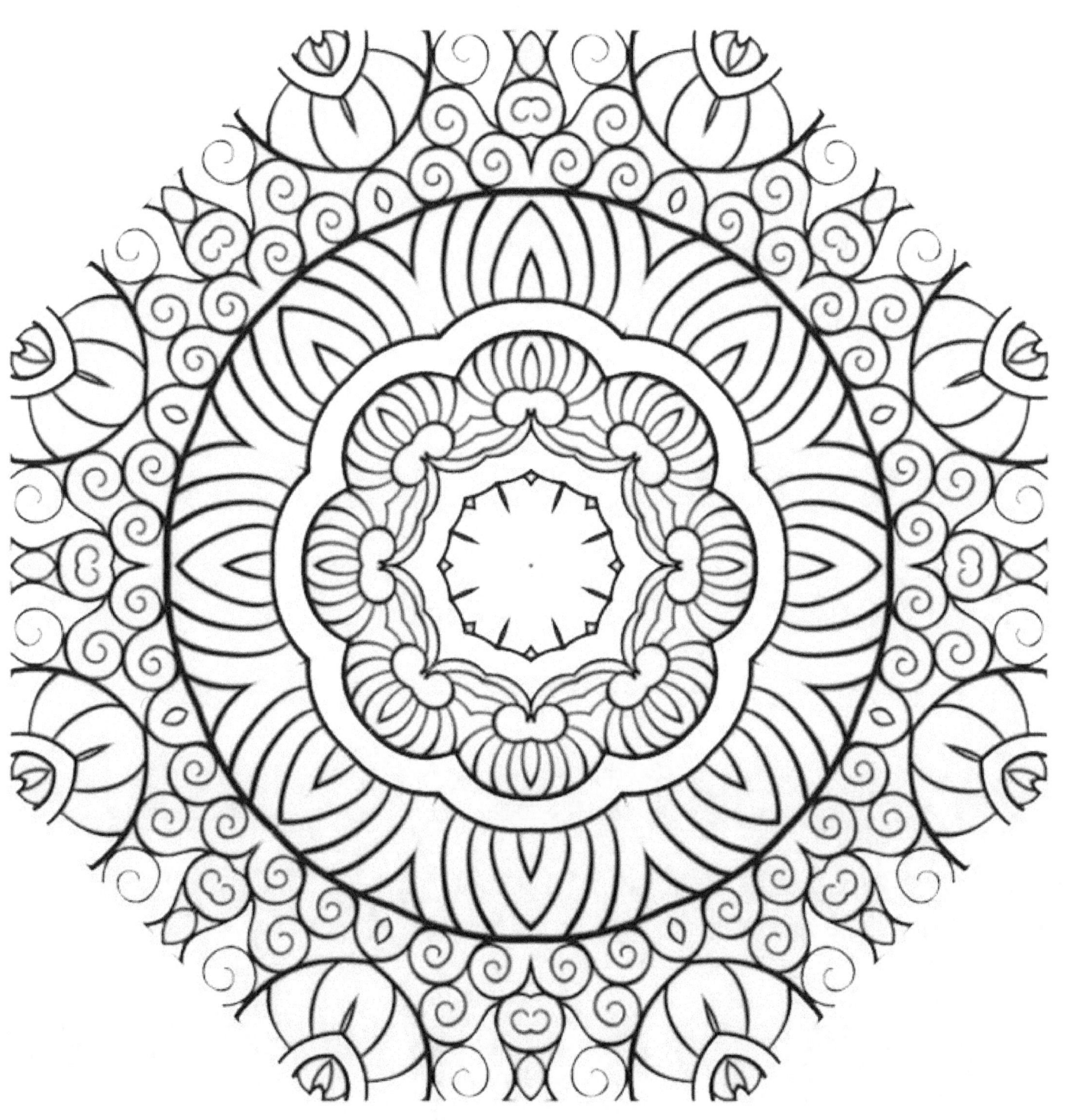

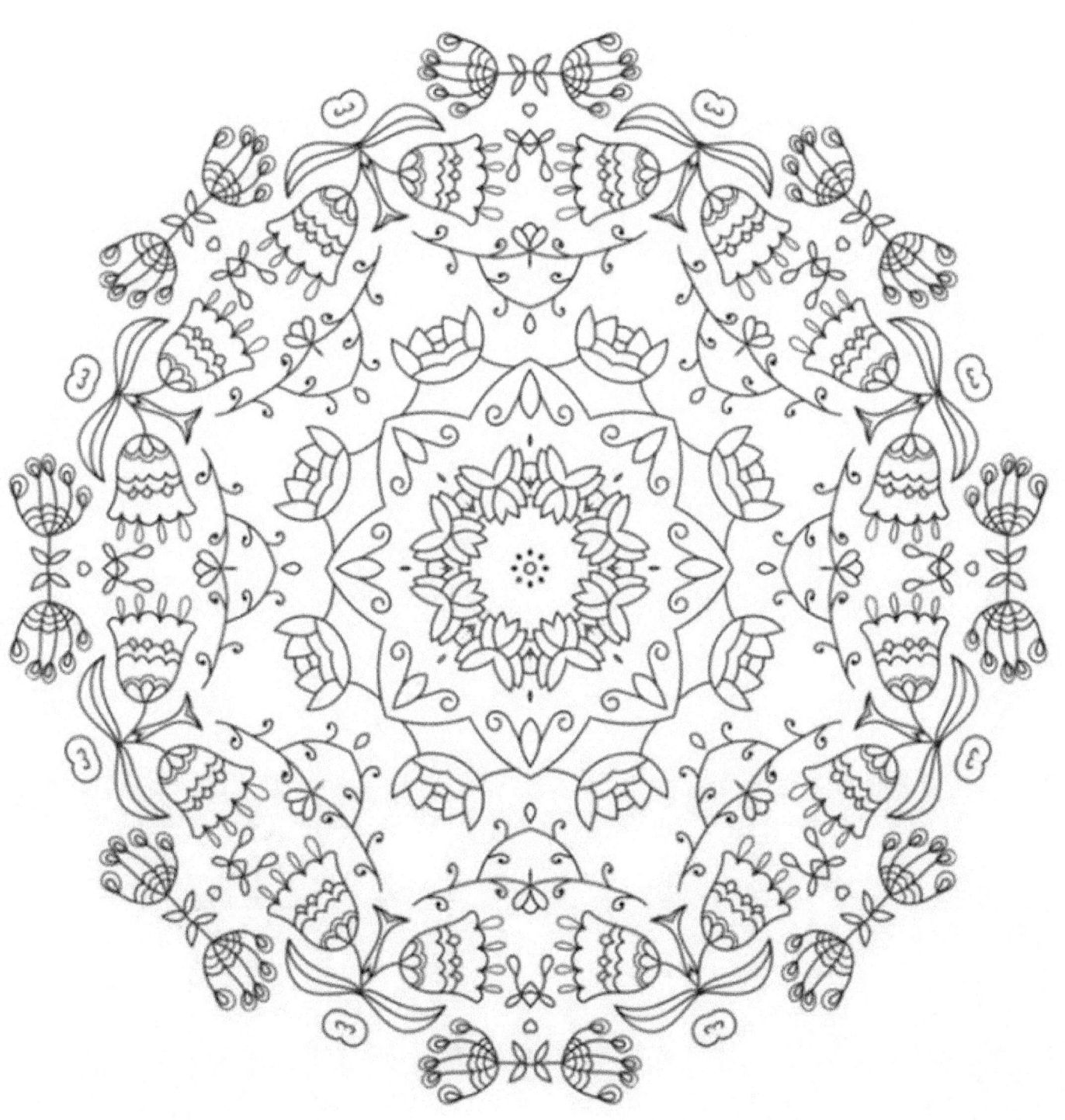

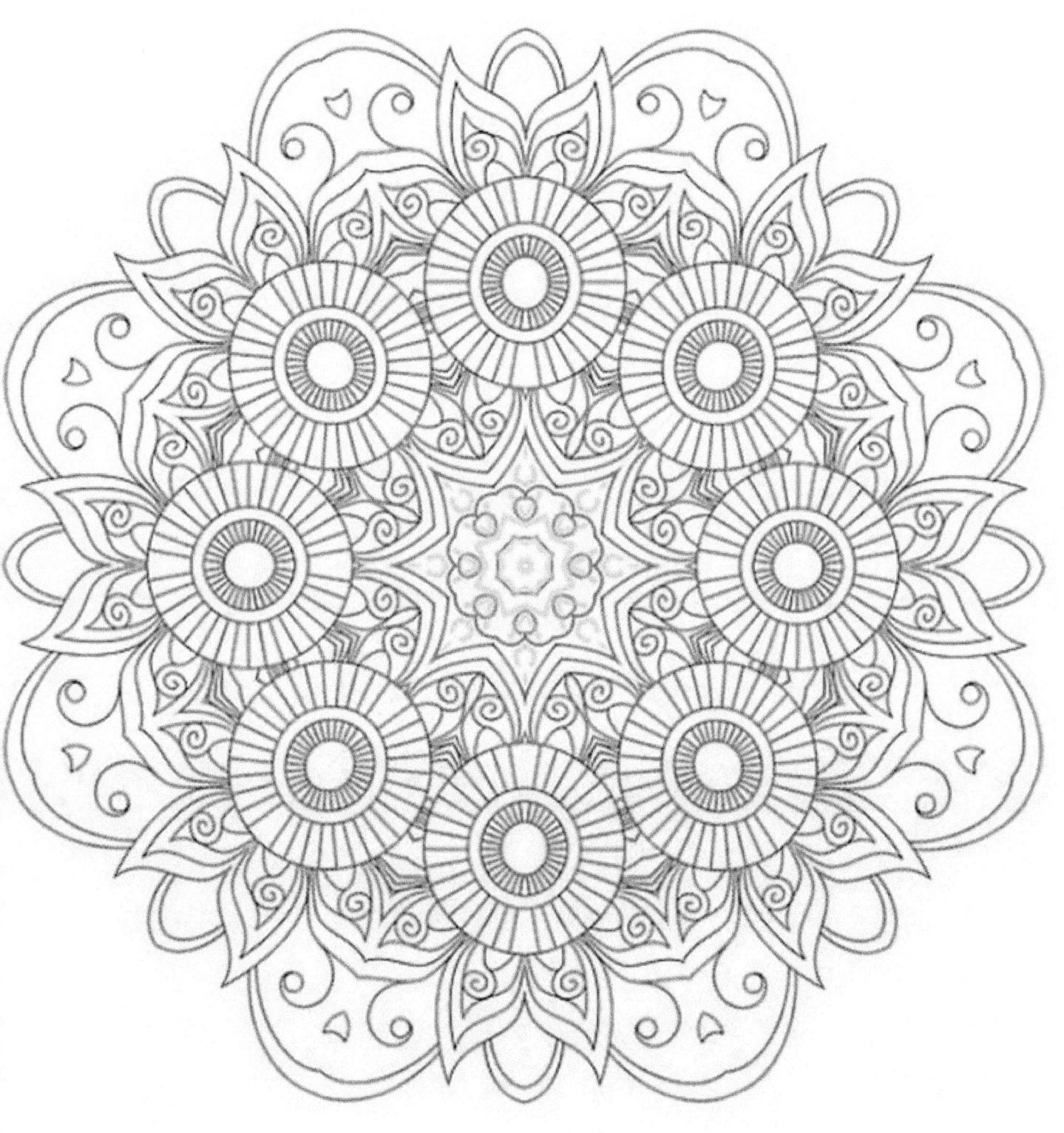

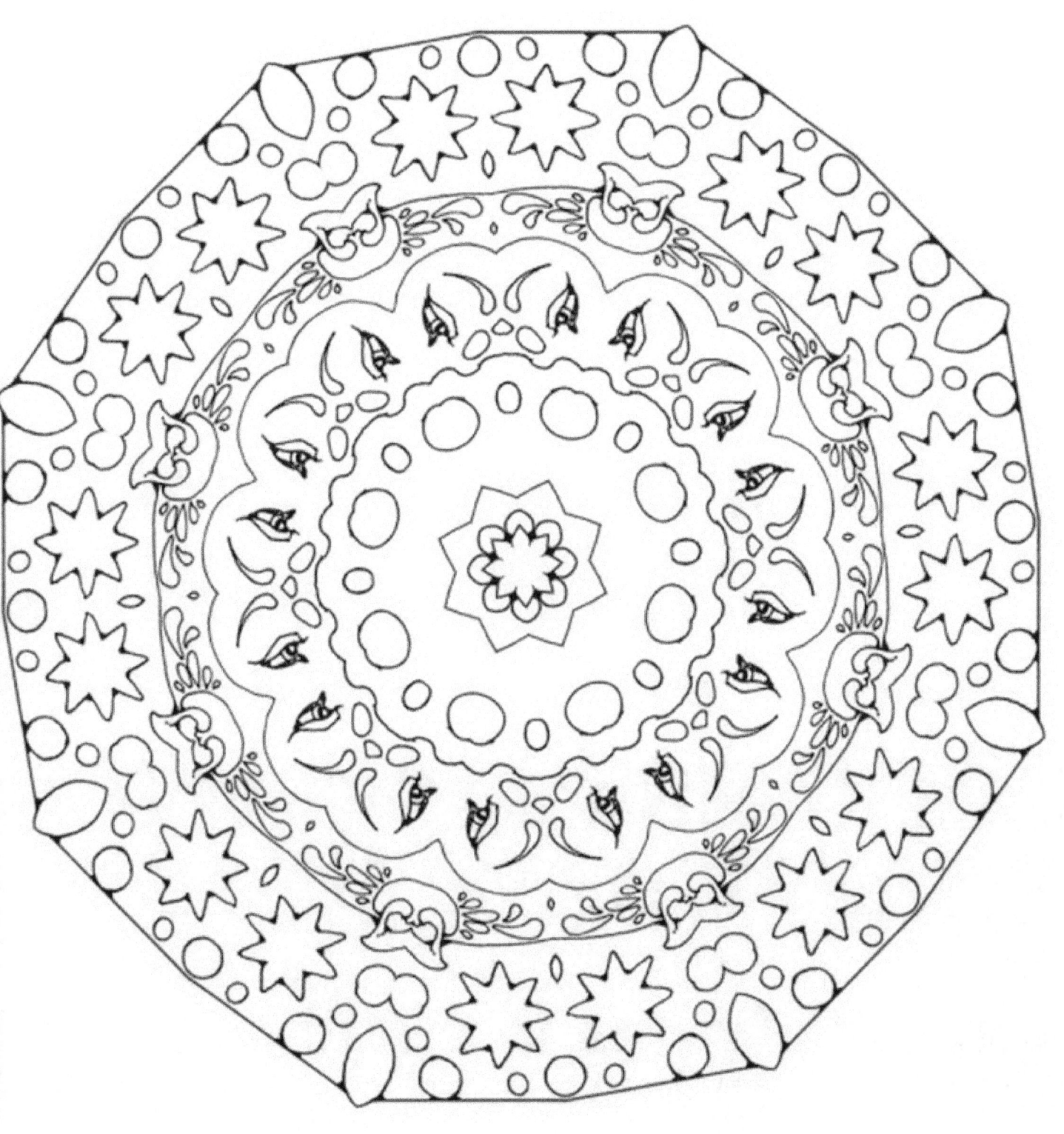

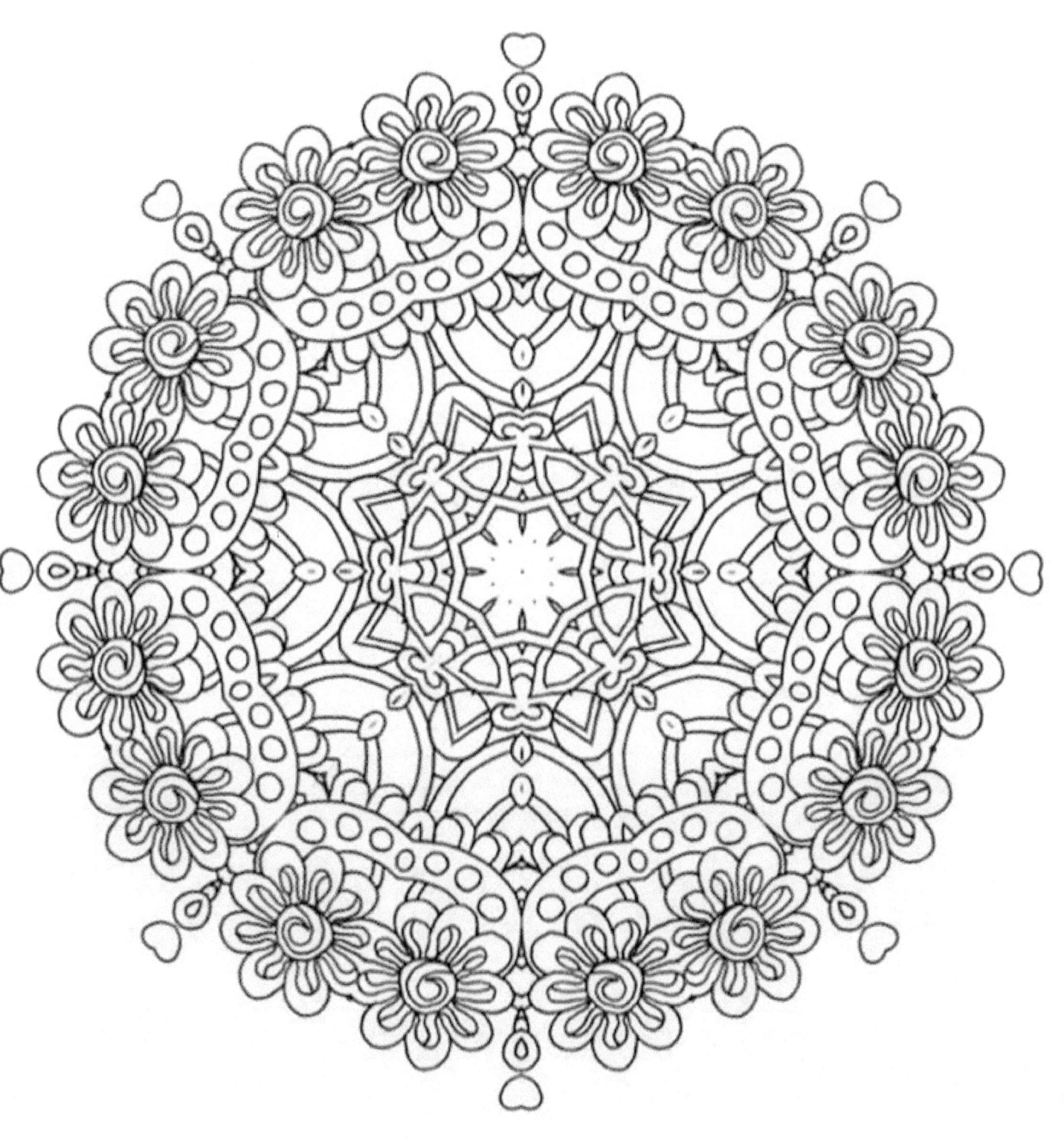

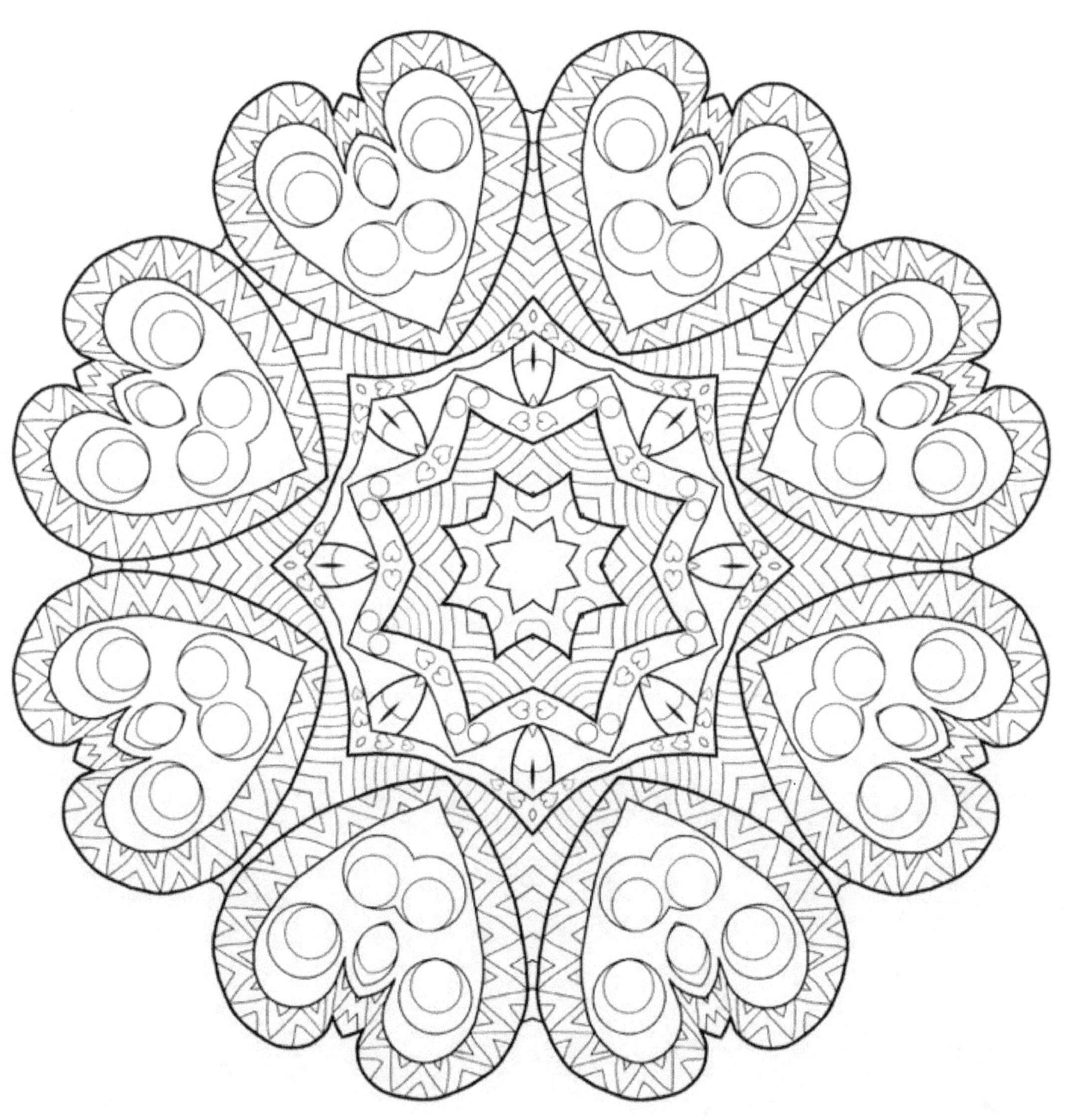

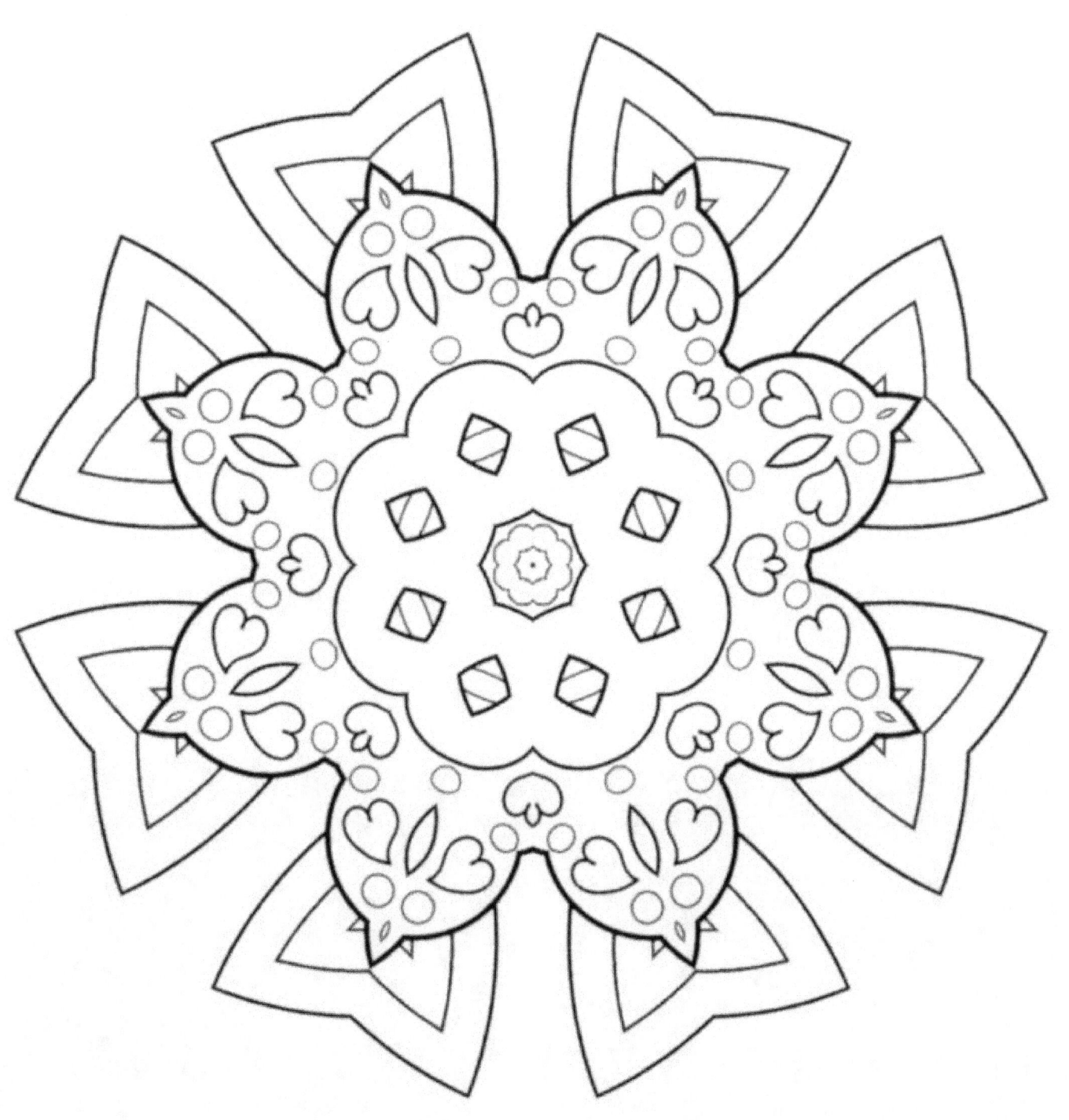

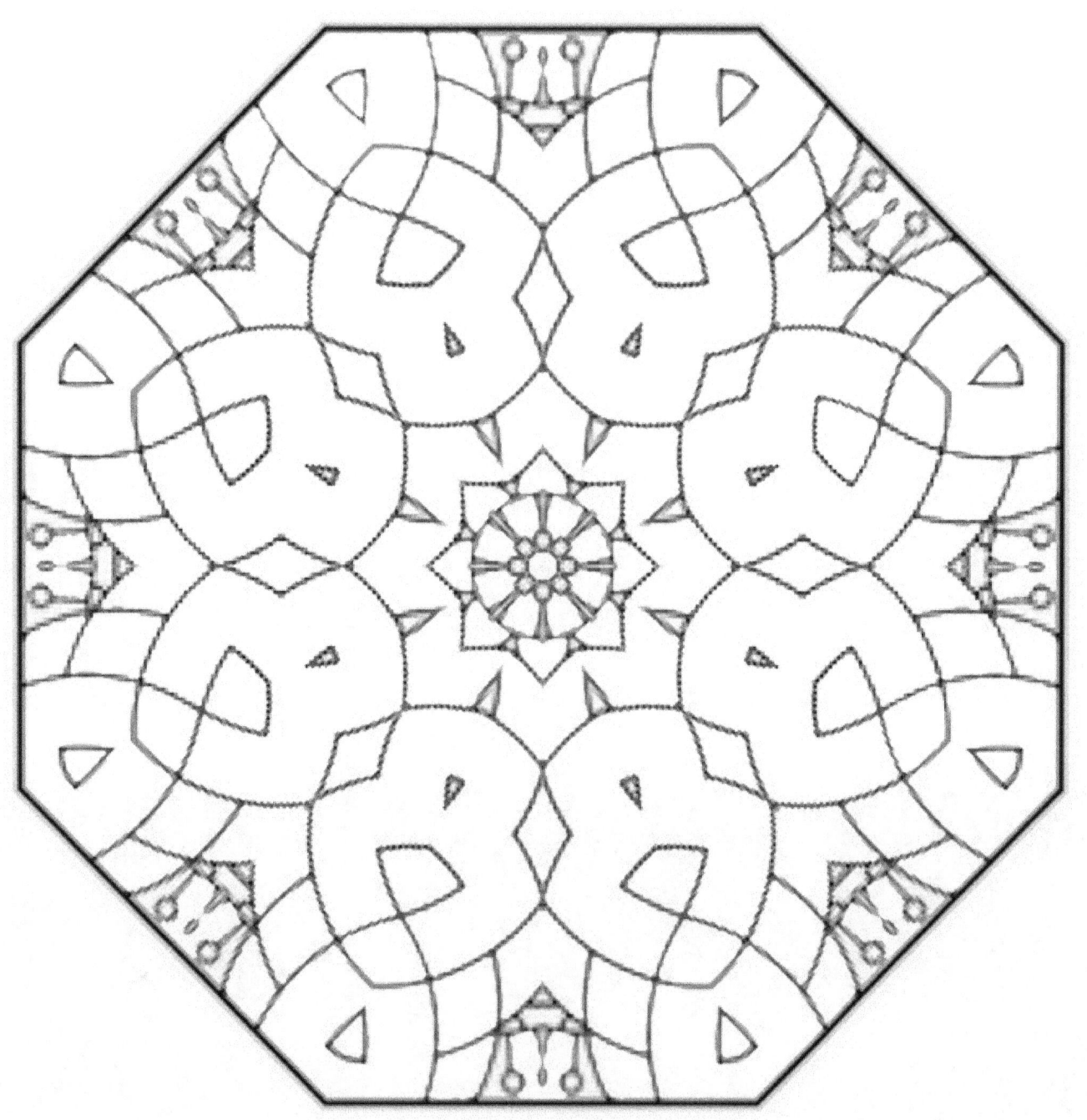

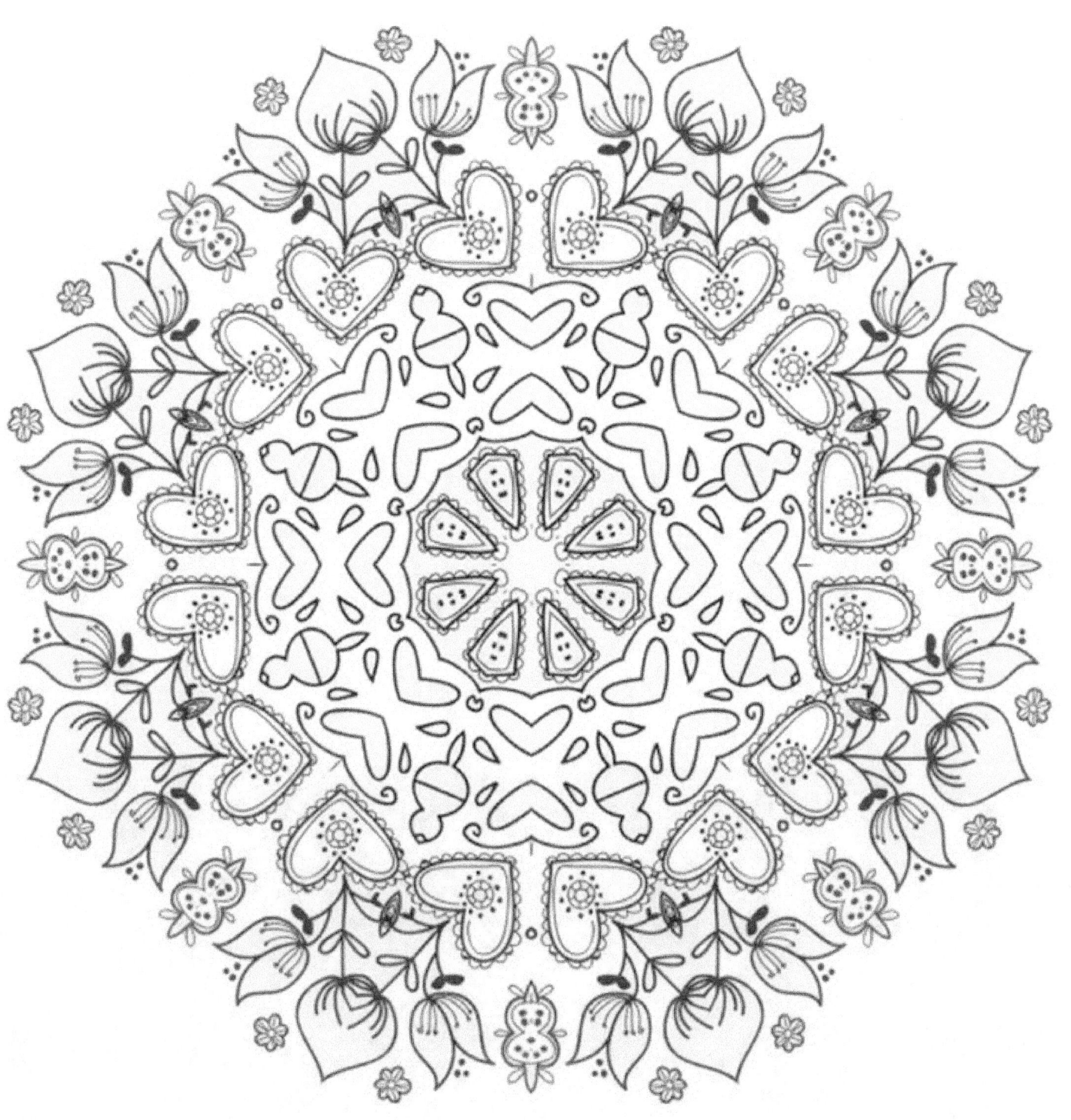

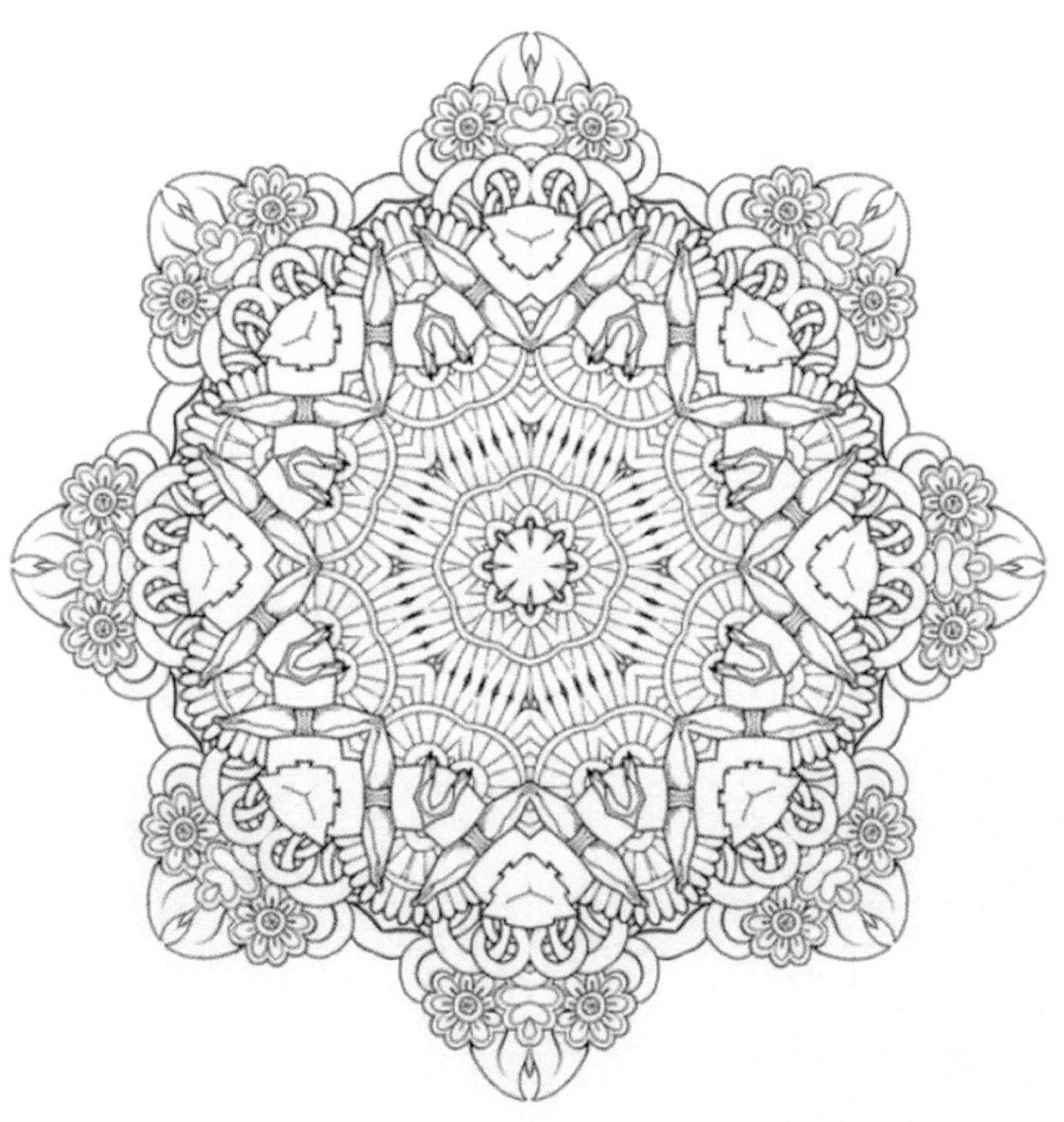

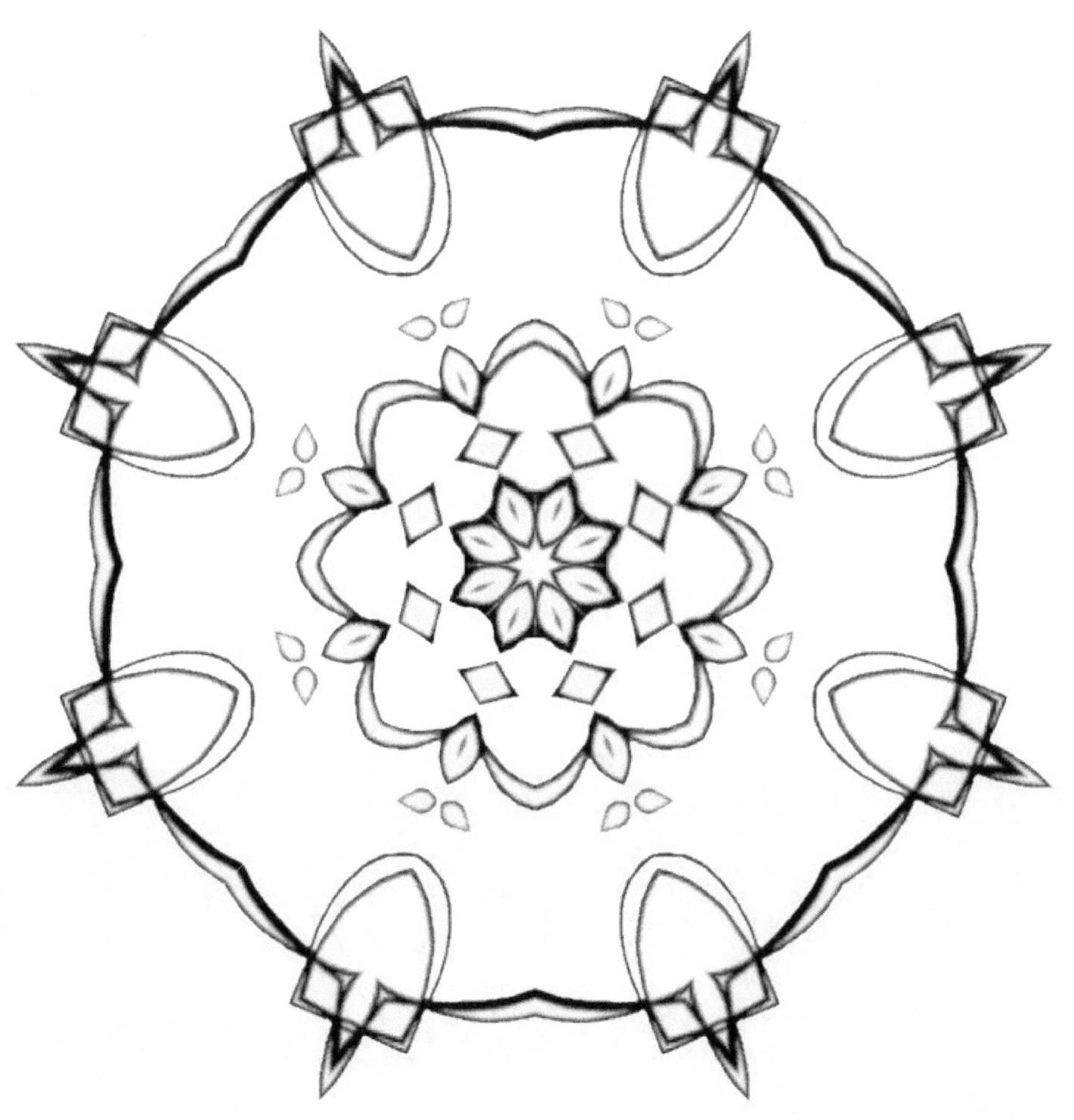

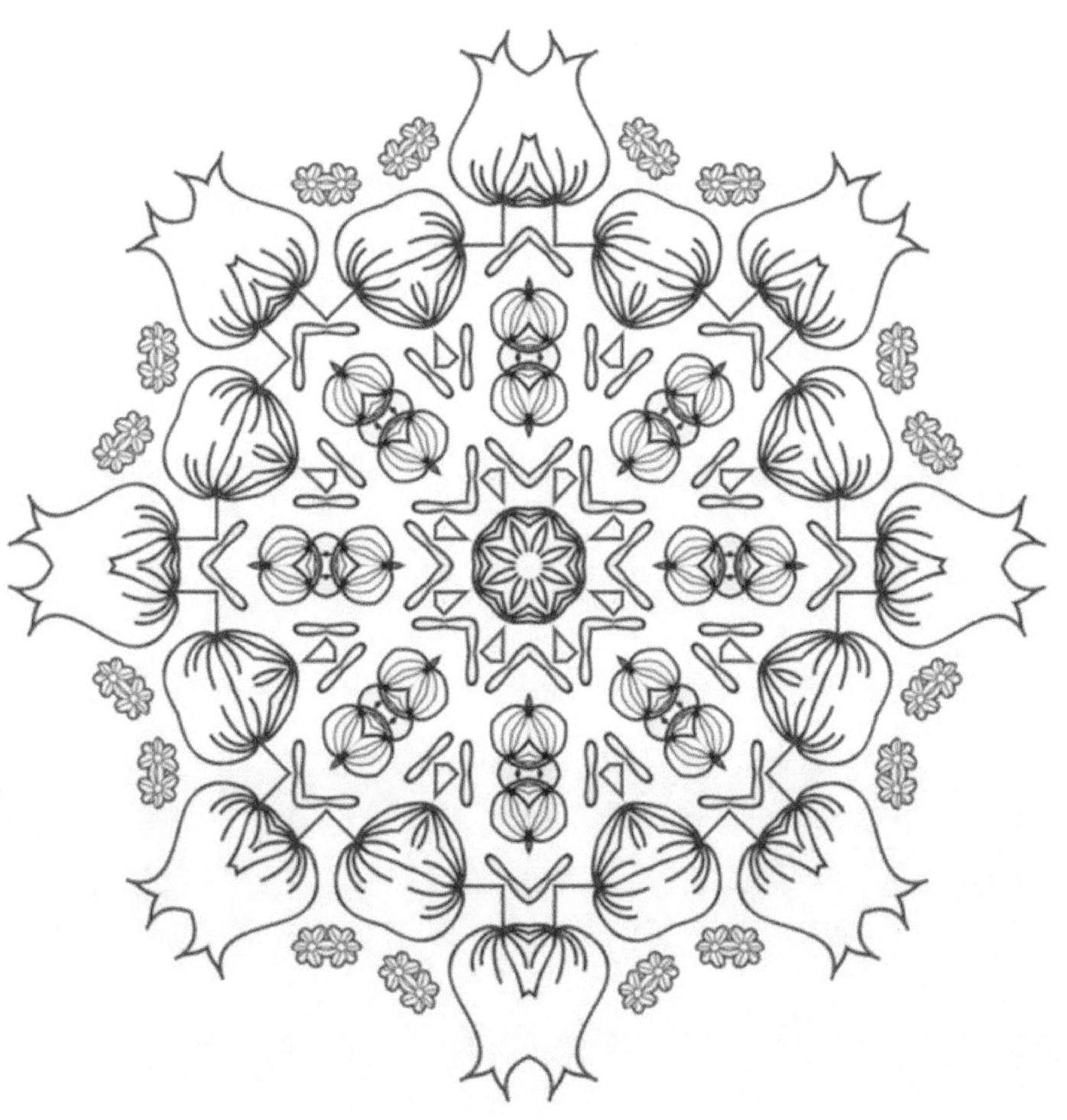

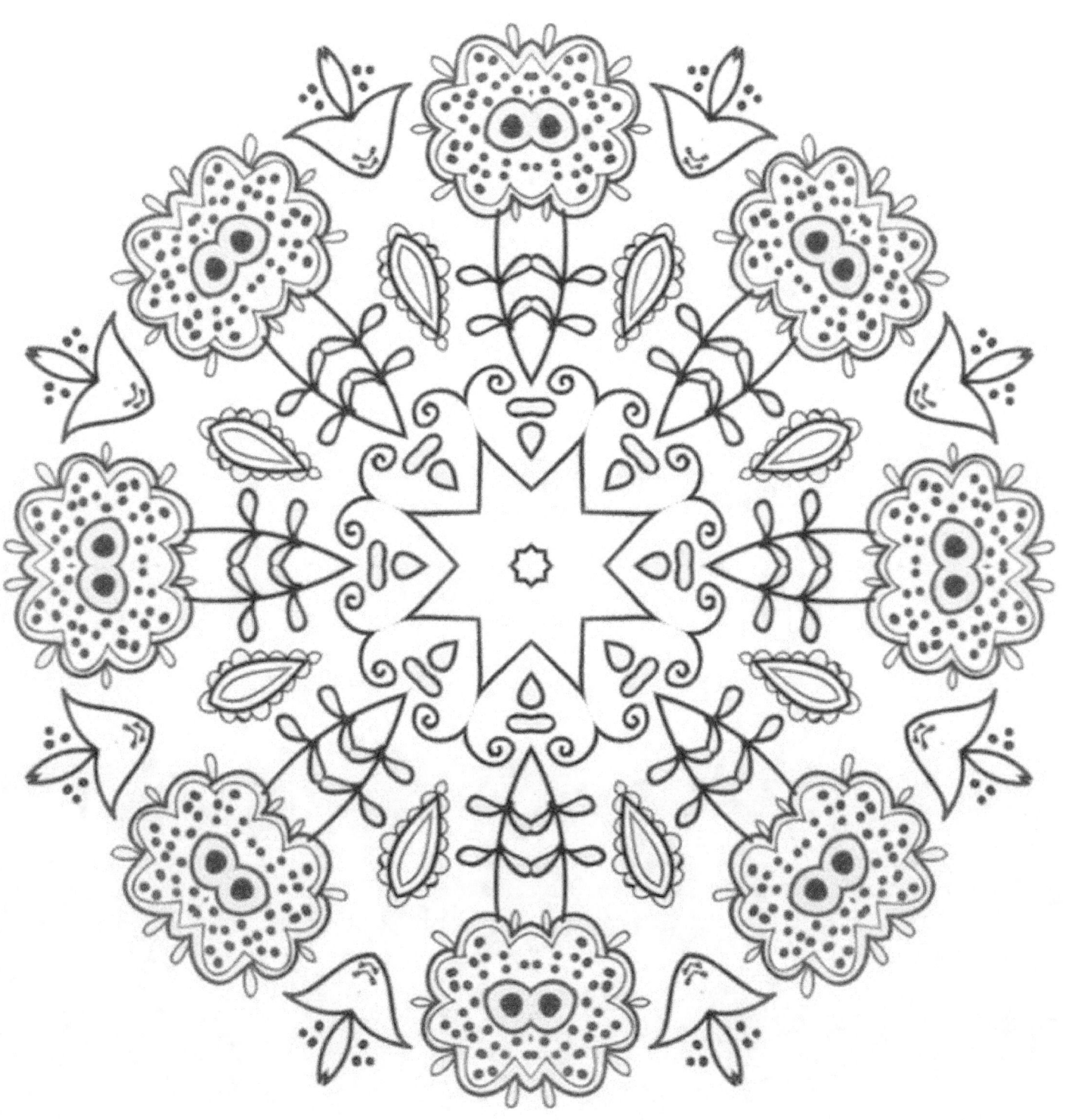

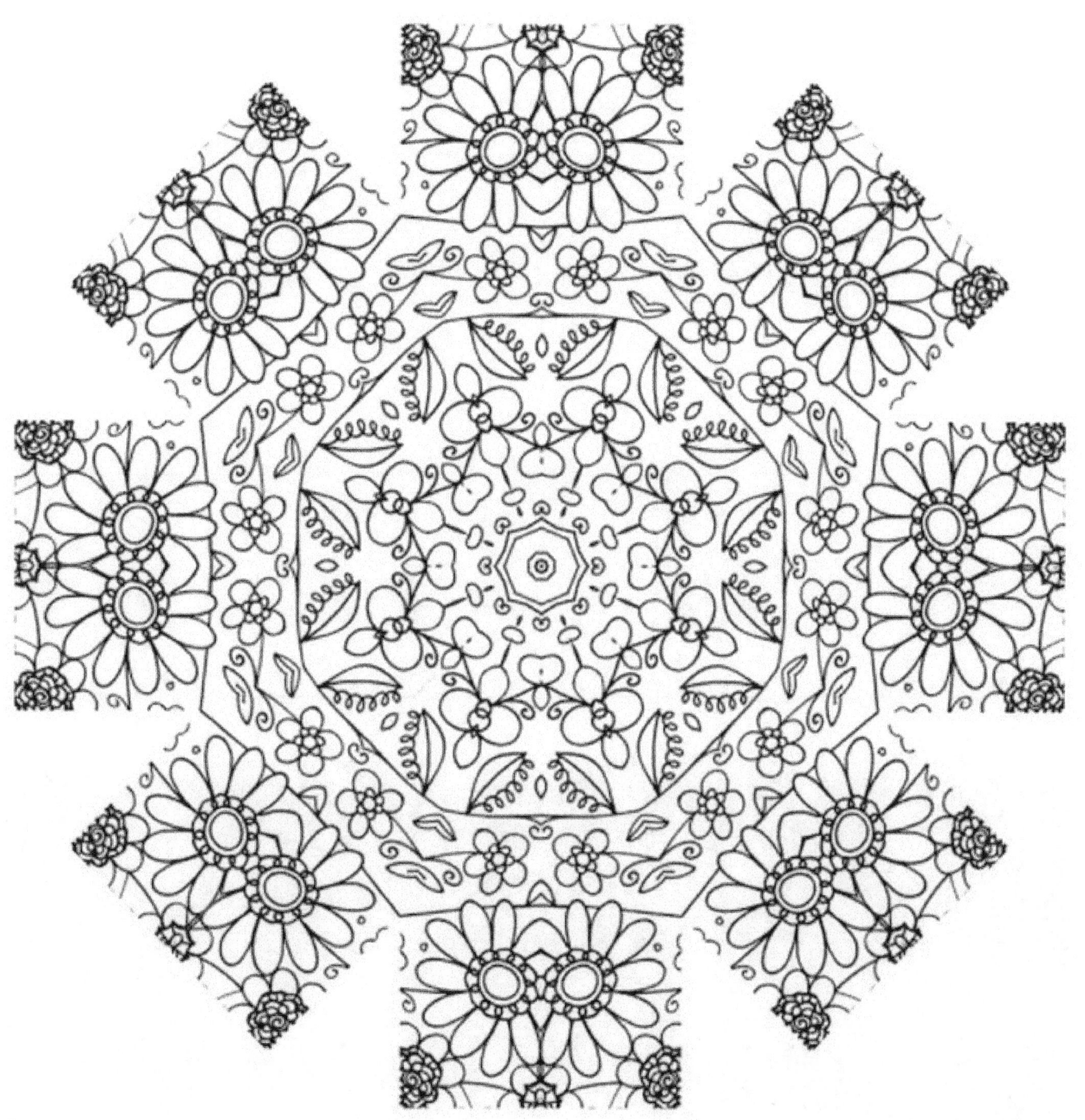

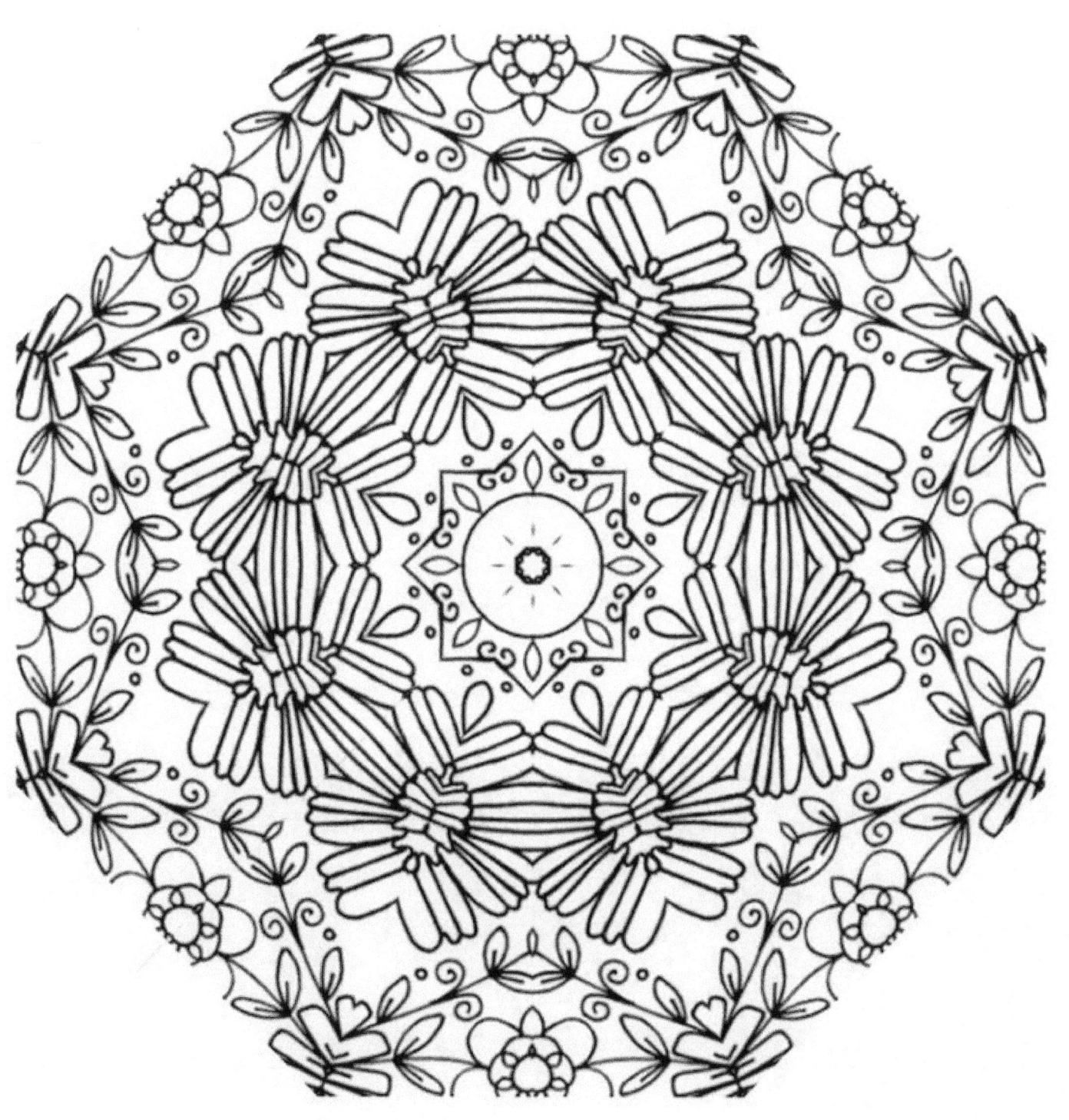

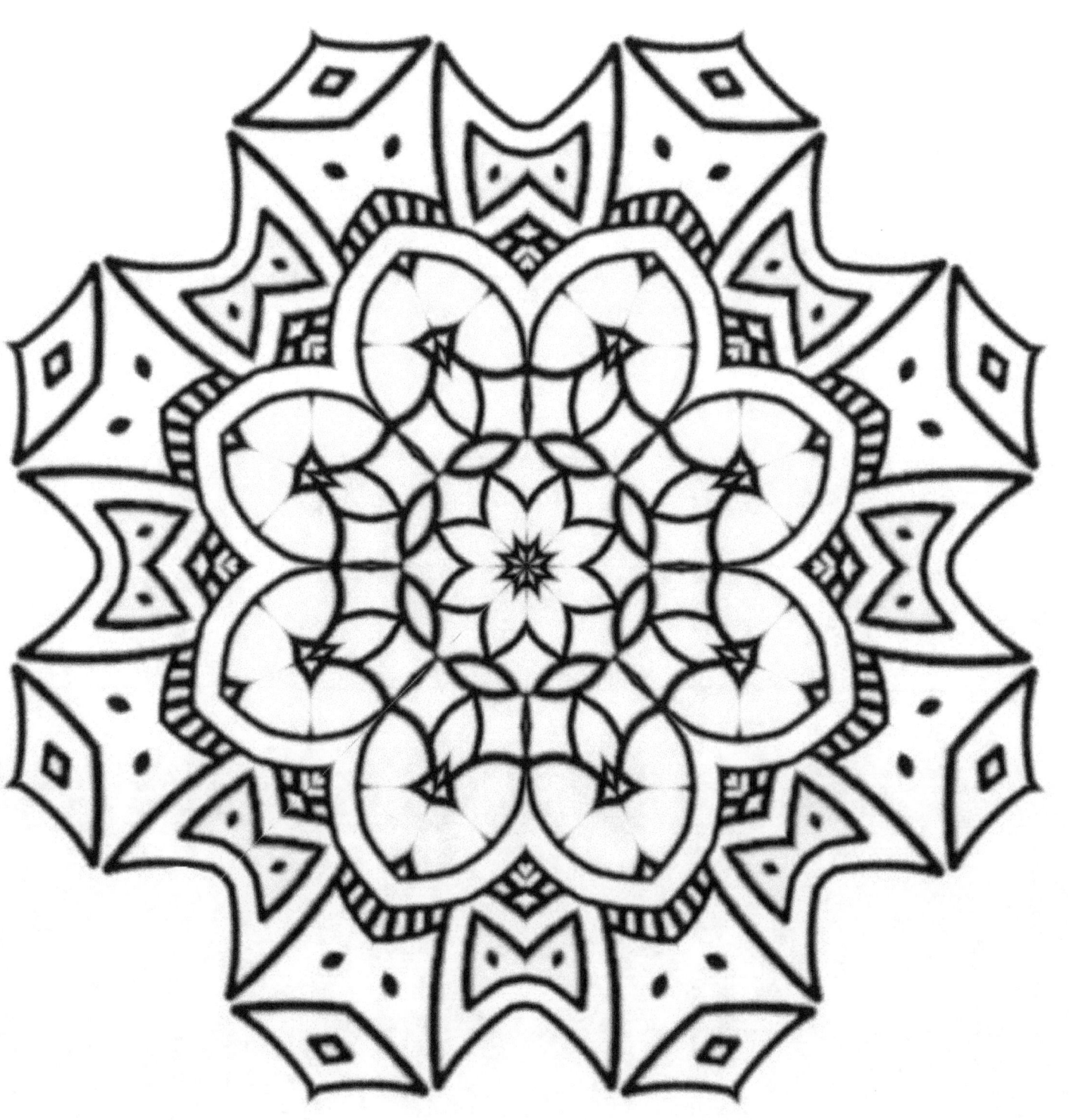

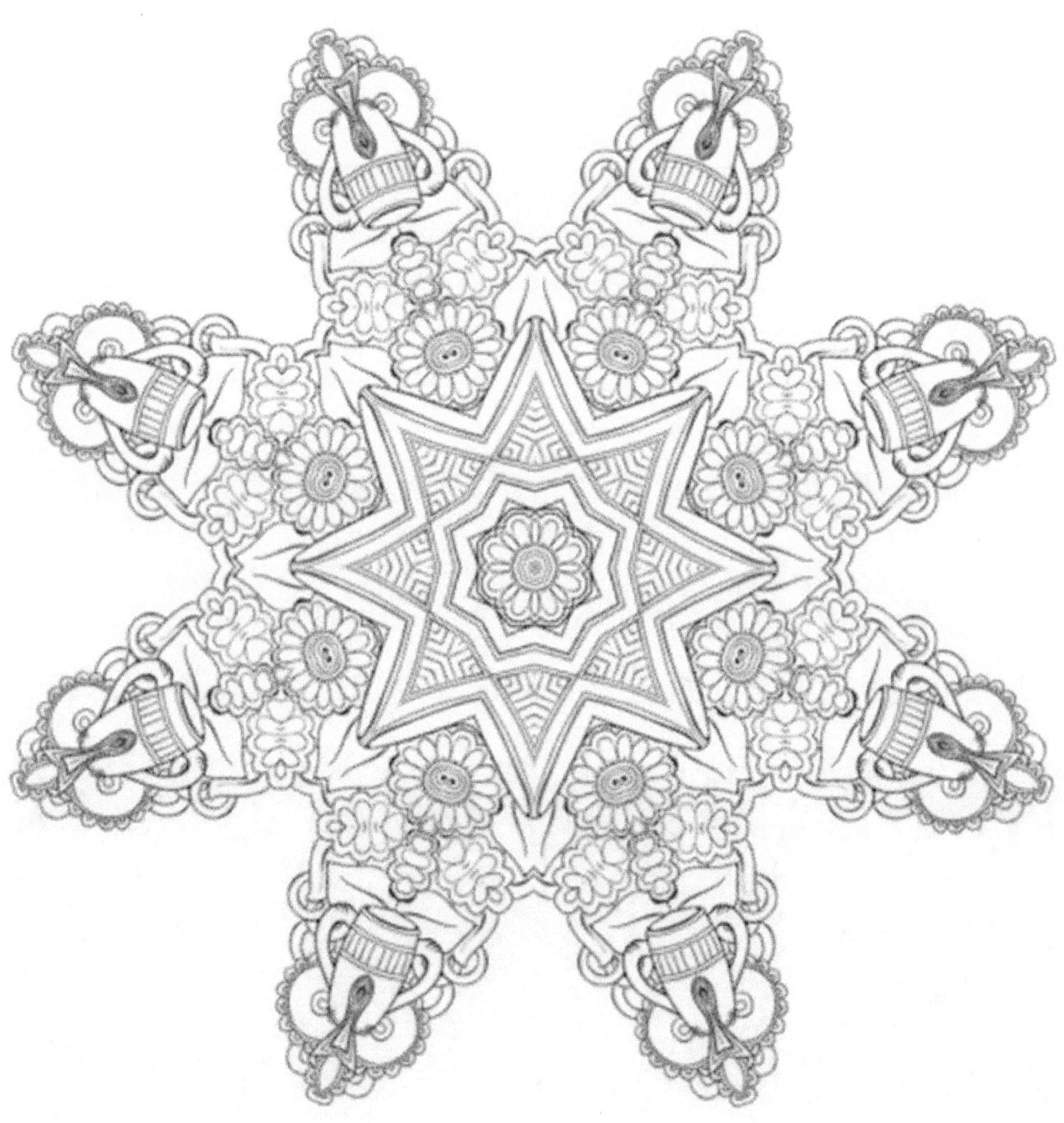

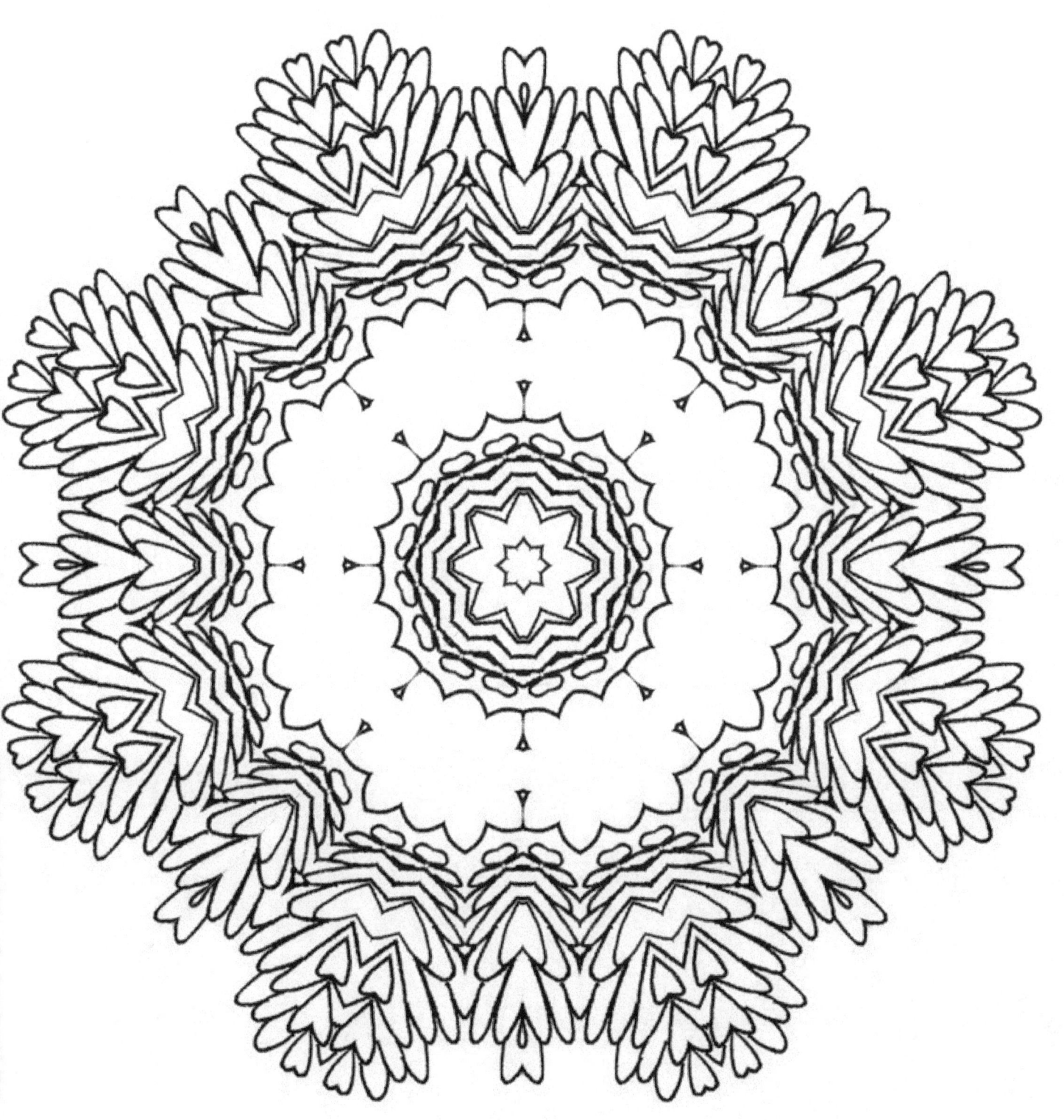

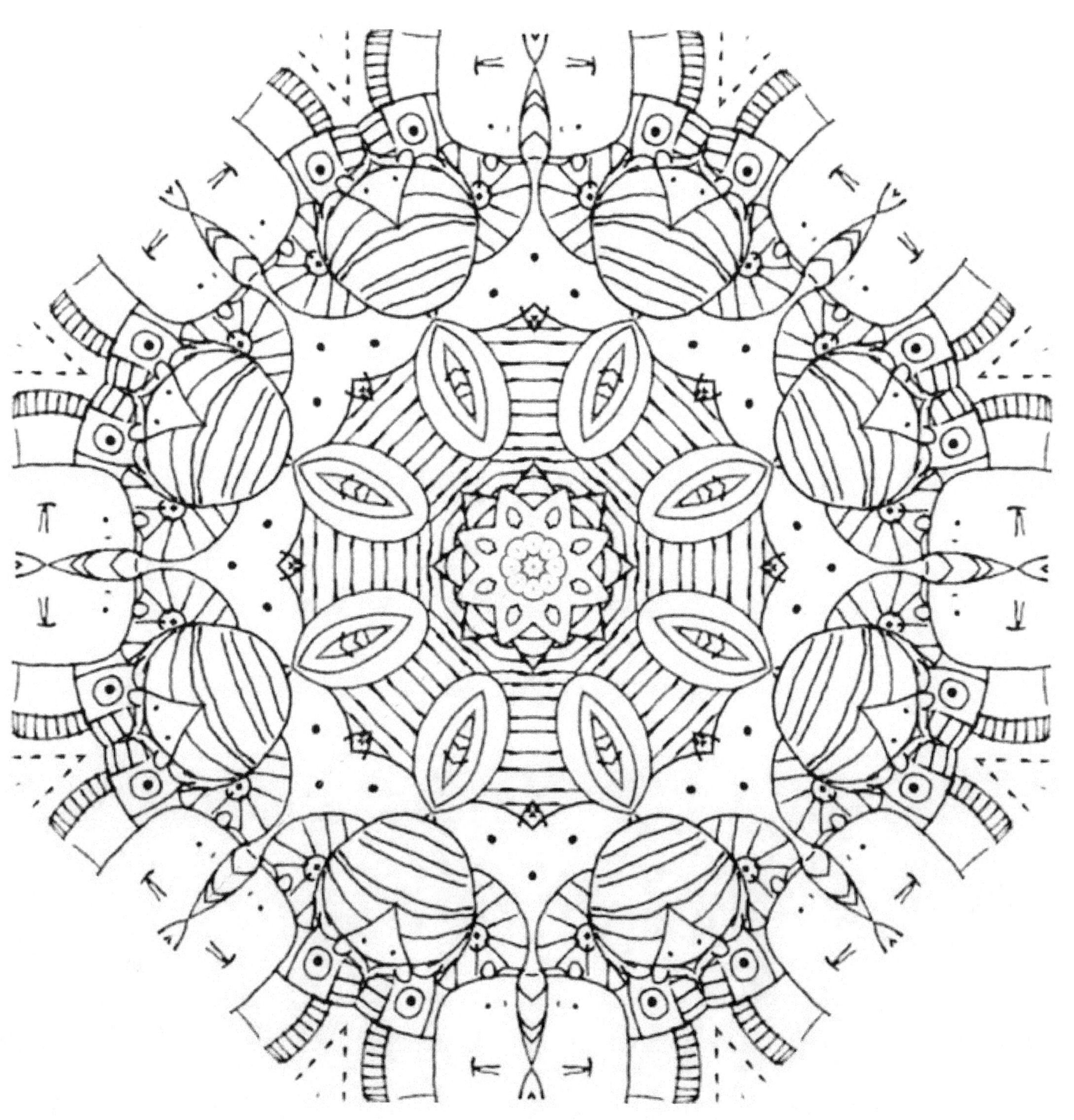

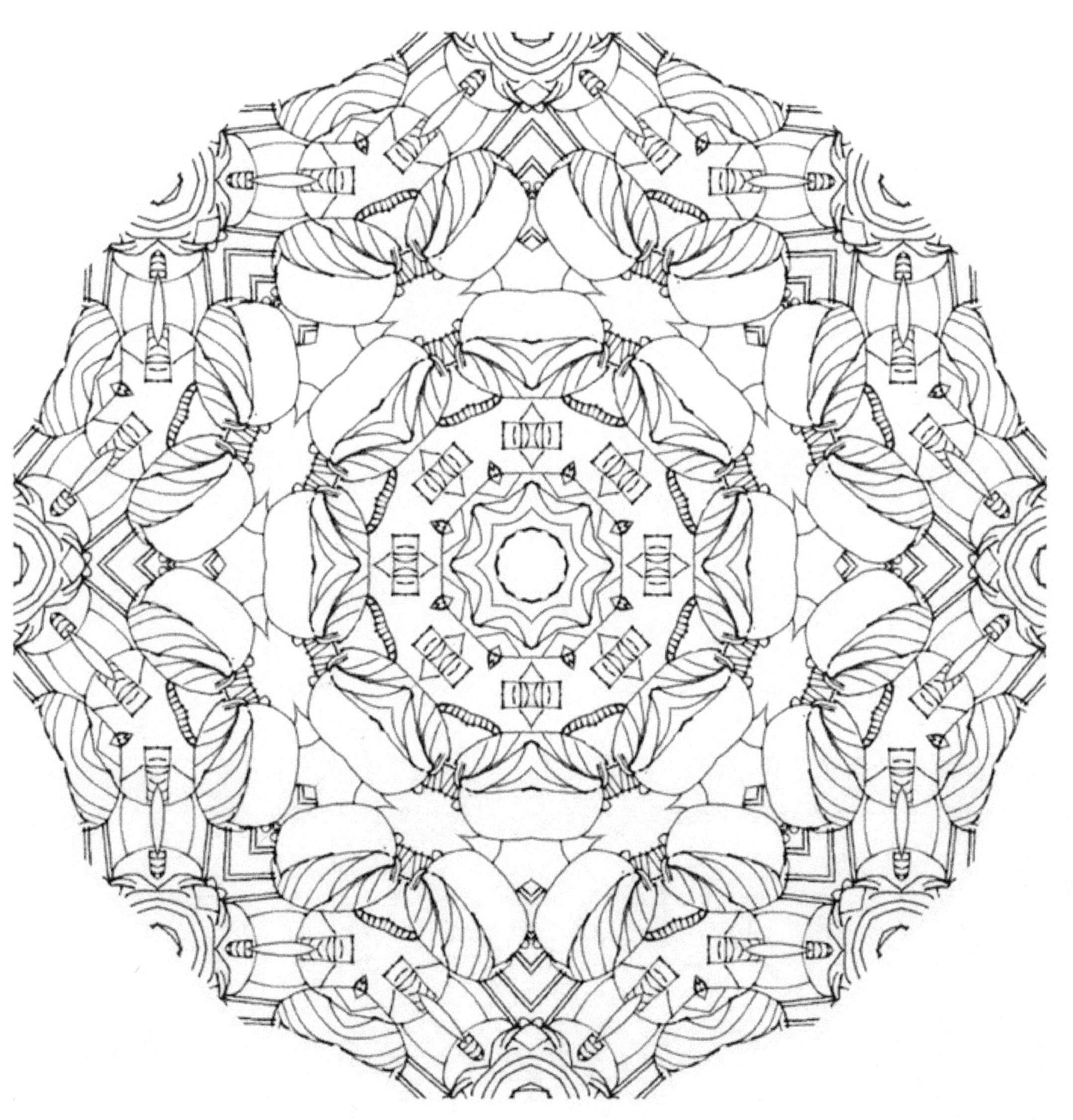

www.ingramcontent.com/pod-product-compliance
Lightning Source LLC
Chambersburg PA
CBHW080617190526
45169CB00009B/3209